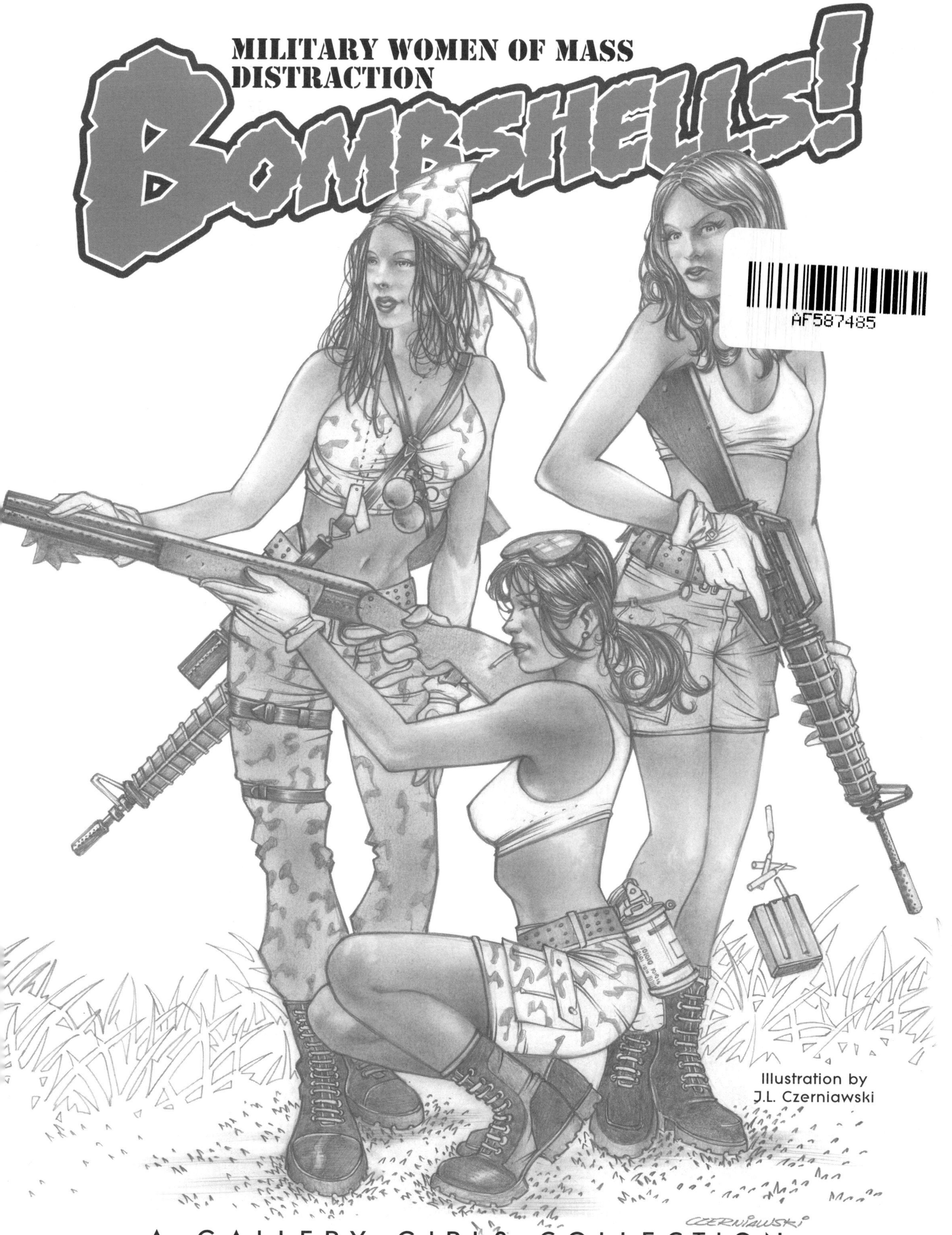

A GALLERY GIRLS COLLECTION

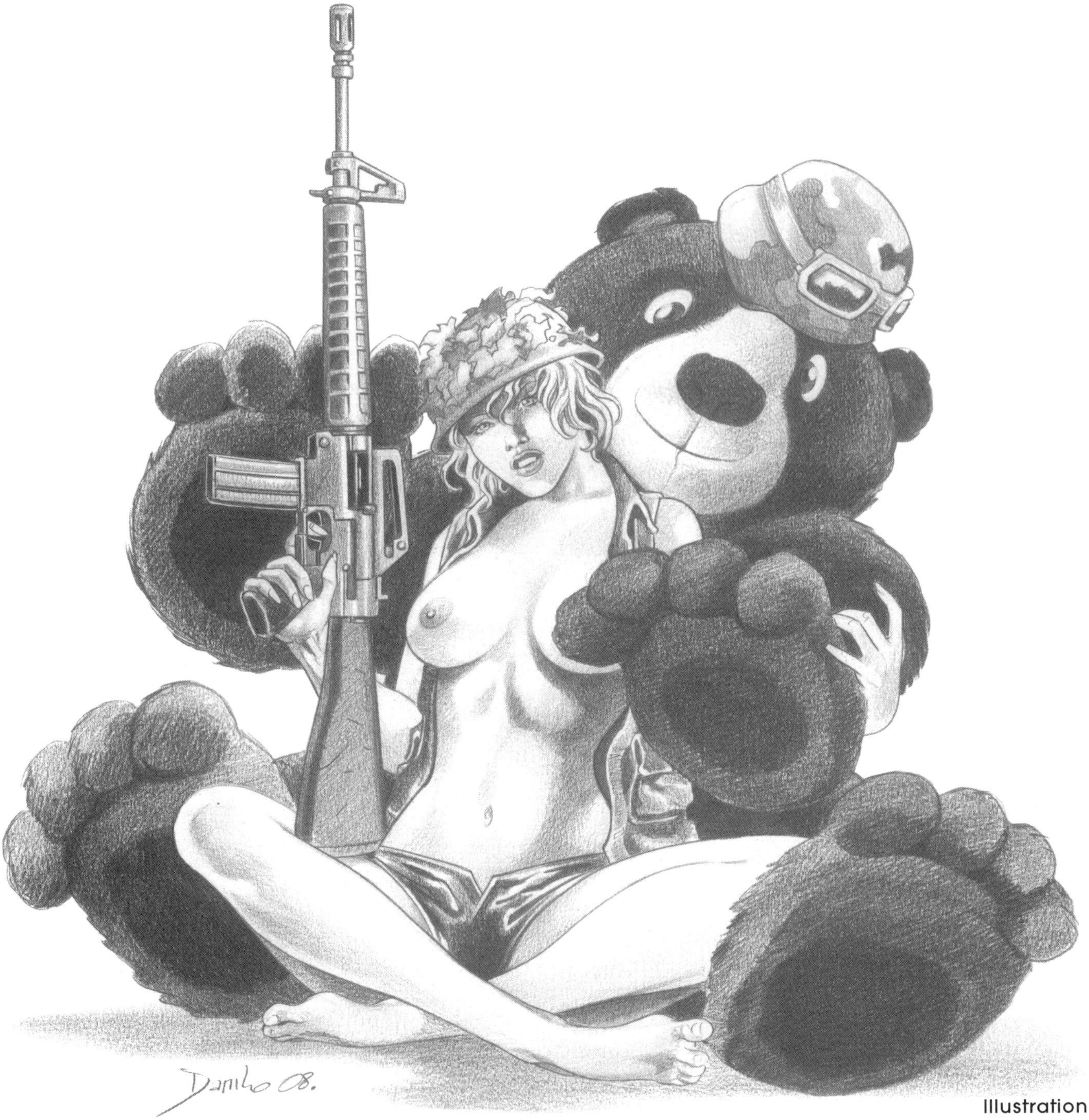

Illustration by
Danilo Guida

BOMBSHELLS!

Volume One

Book design by Grassy Knoll Studios.

Published by
SQP Inc.
PO Box 248 - Columbus, NJ 08022

Sal Quartuccio & Bob Keenan - Publishers

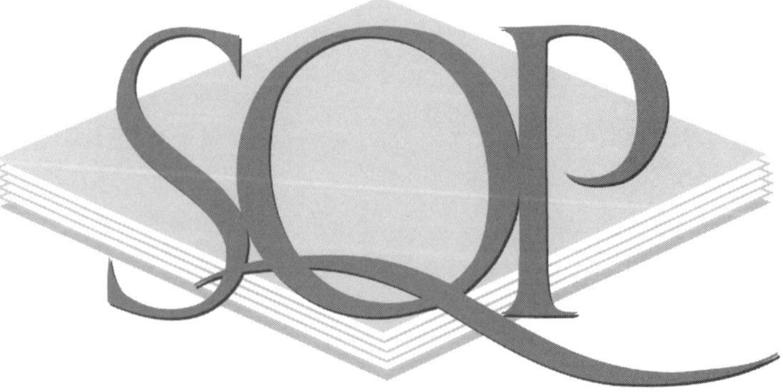

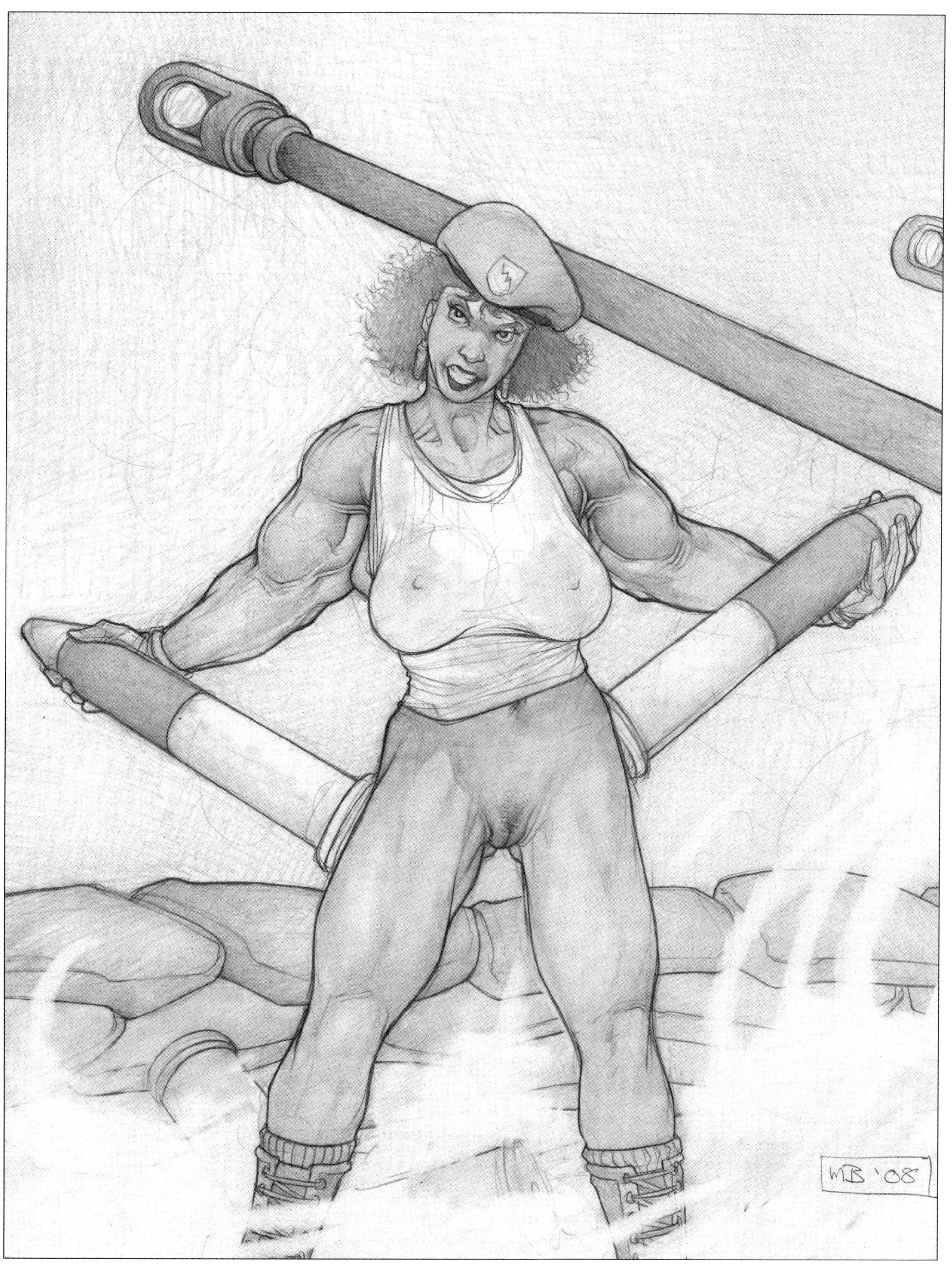

MITCH BYRD

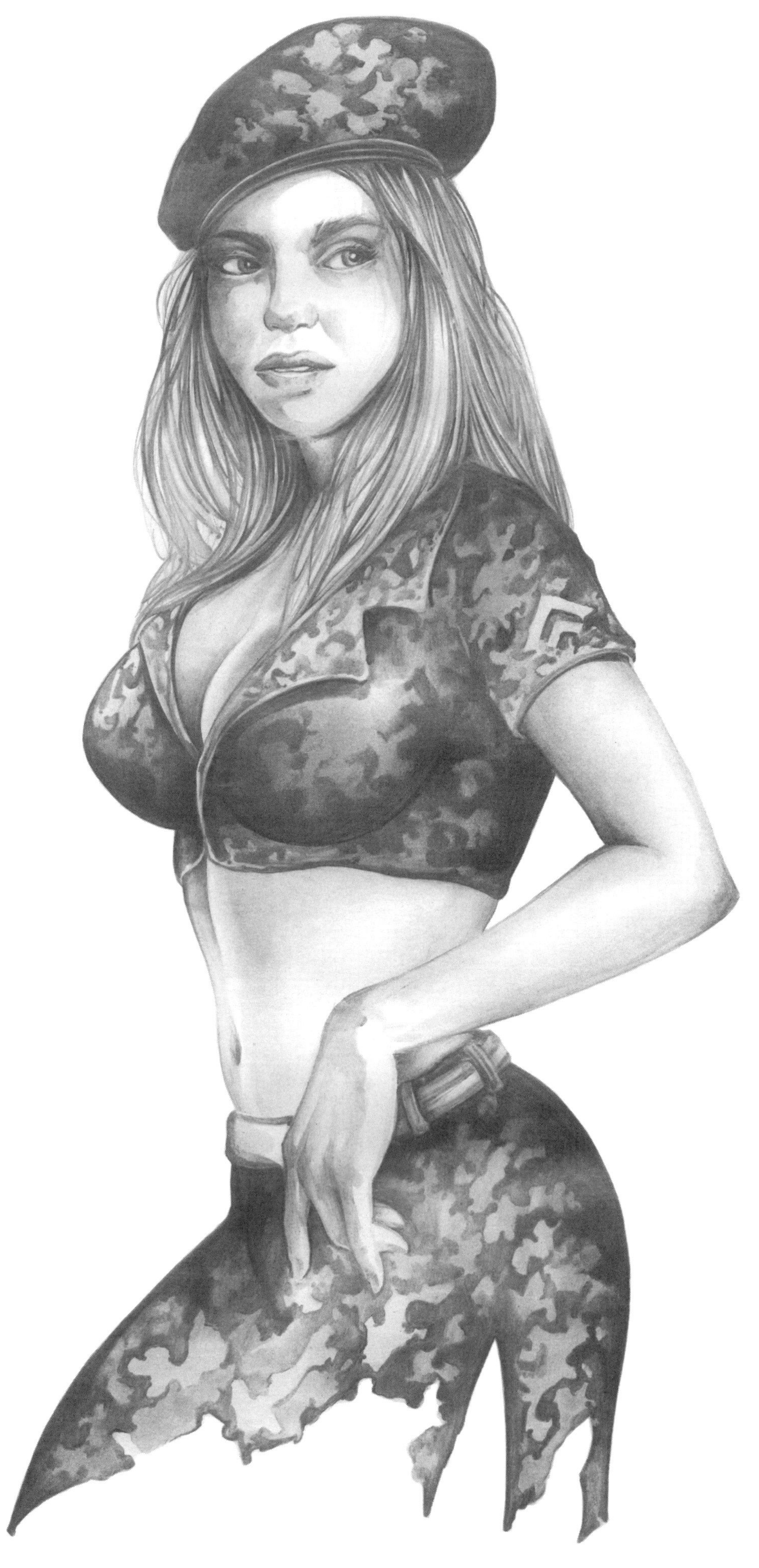

ALDO PEREZ

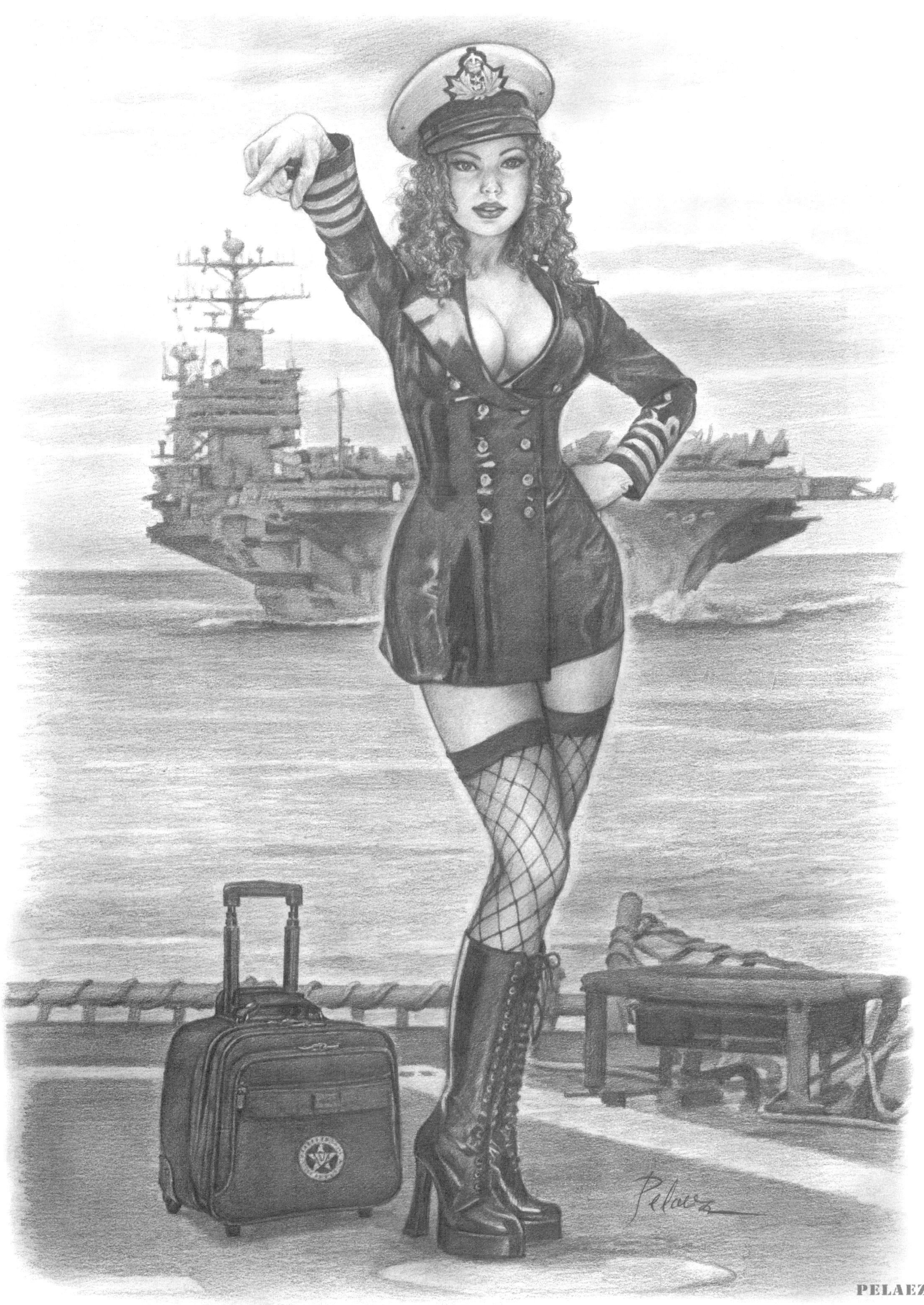

PELAEZ

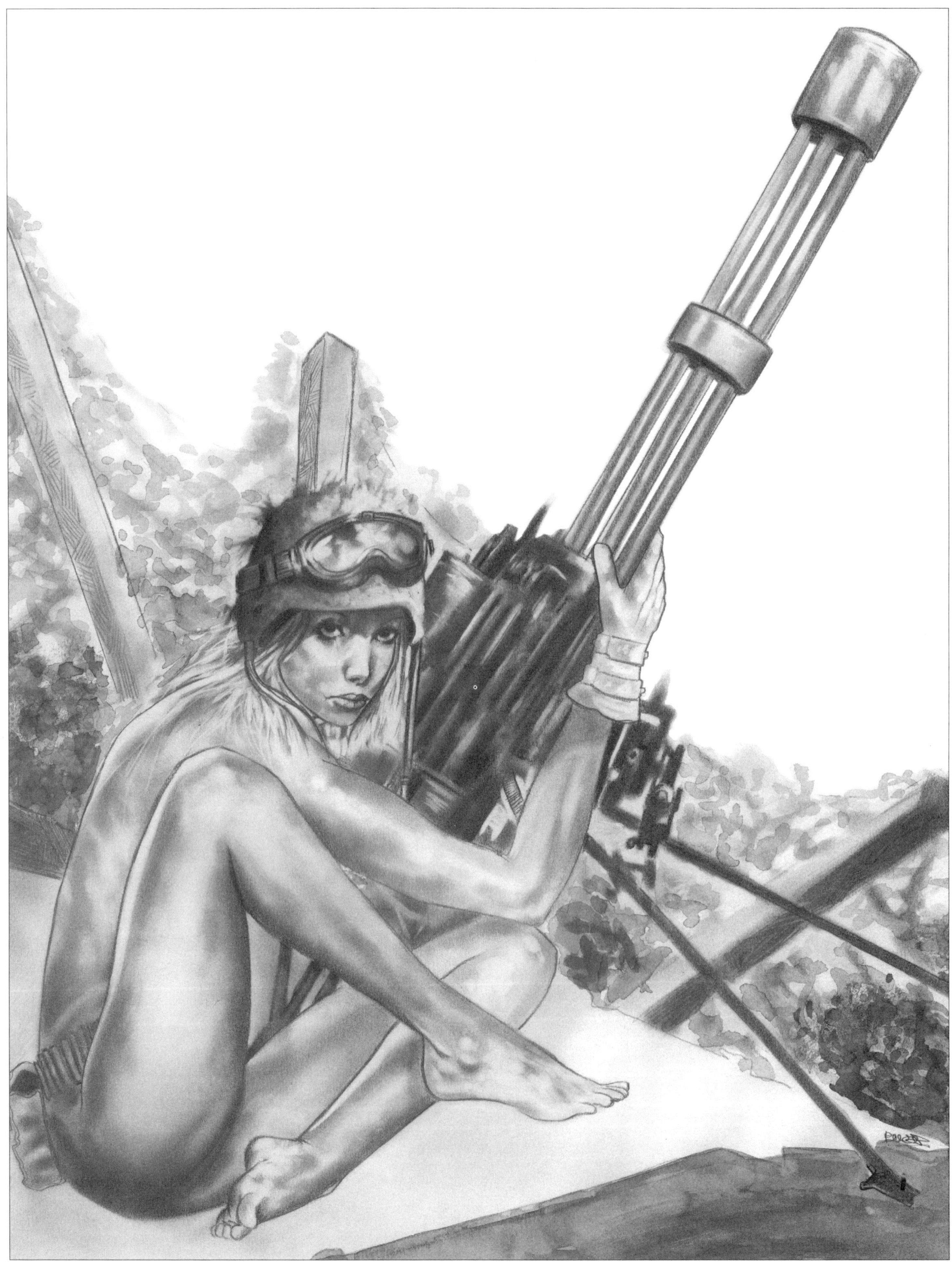

LUIS BUCI

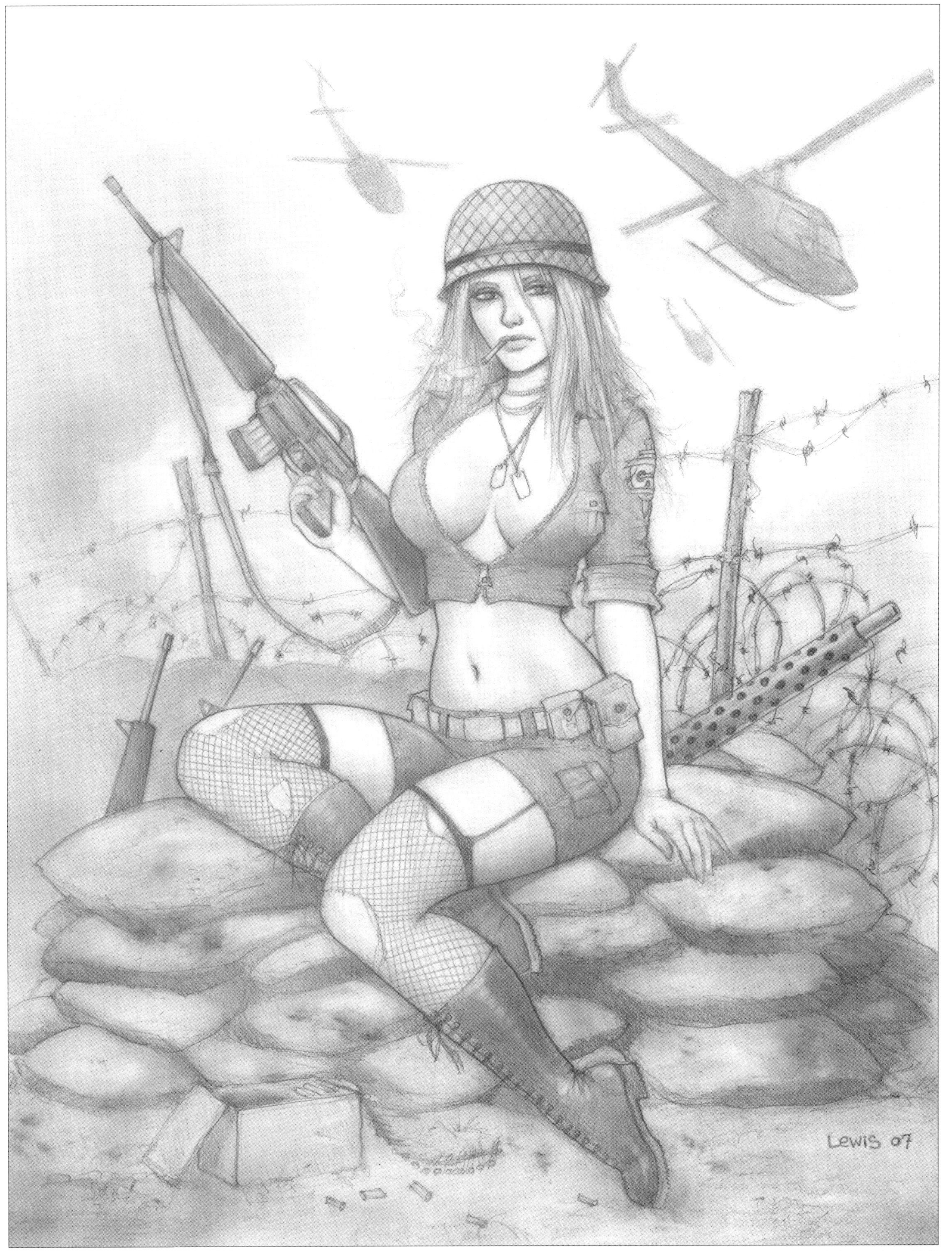

SCOTT LEWIS

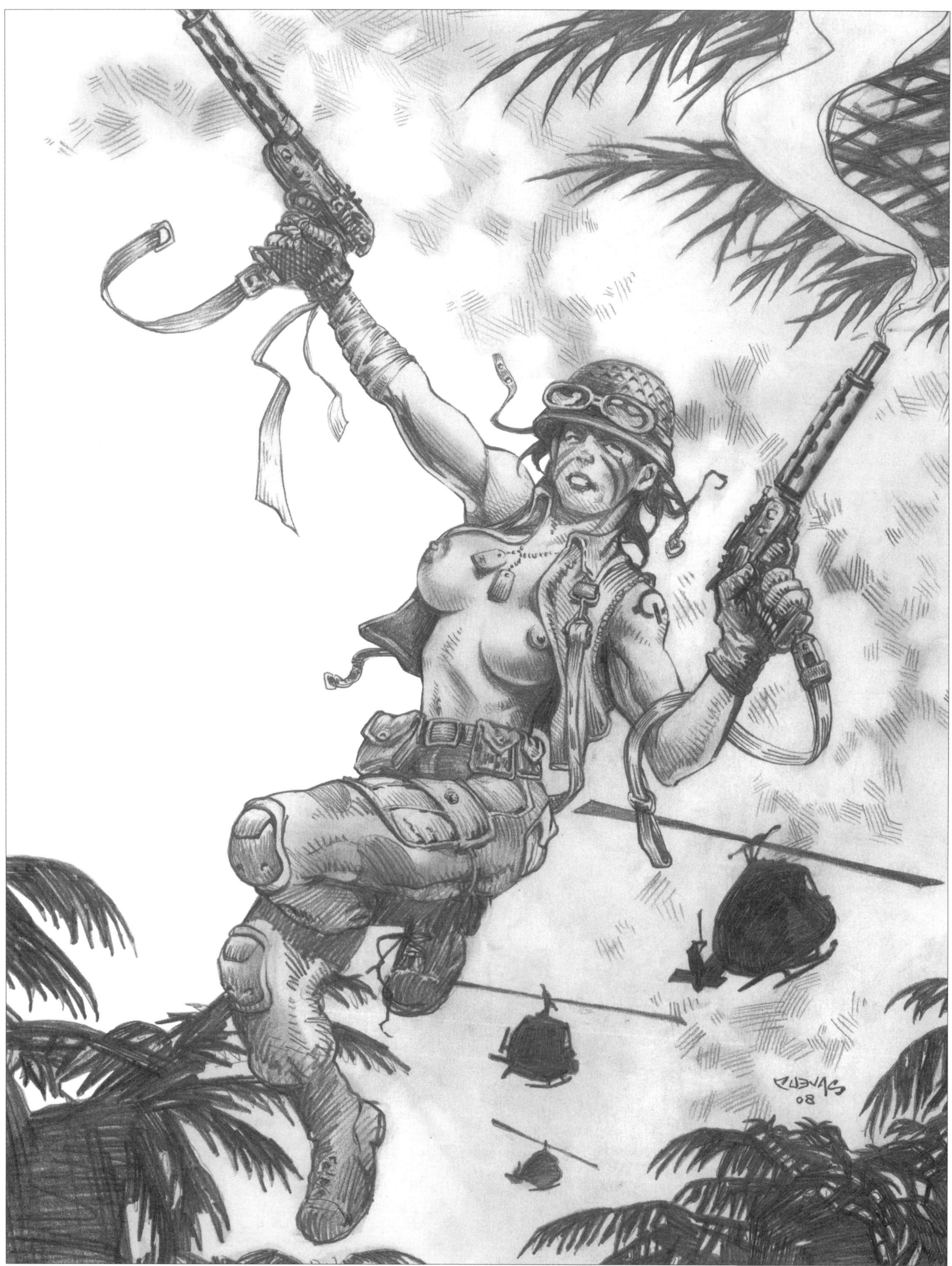

PEDRO CUEVAS

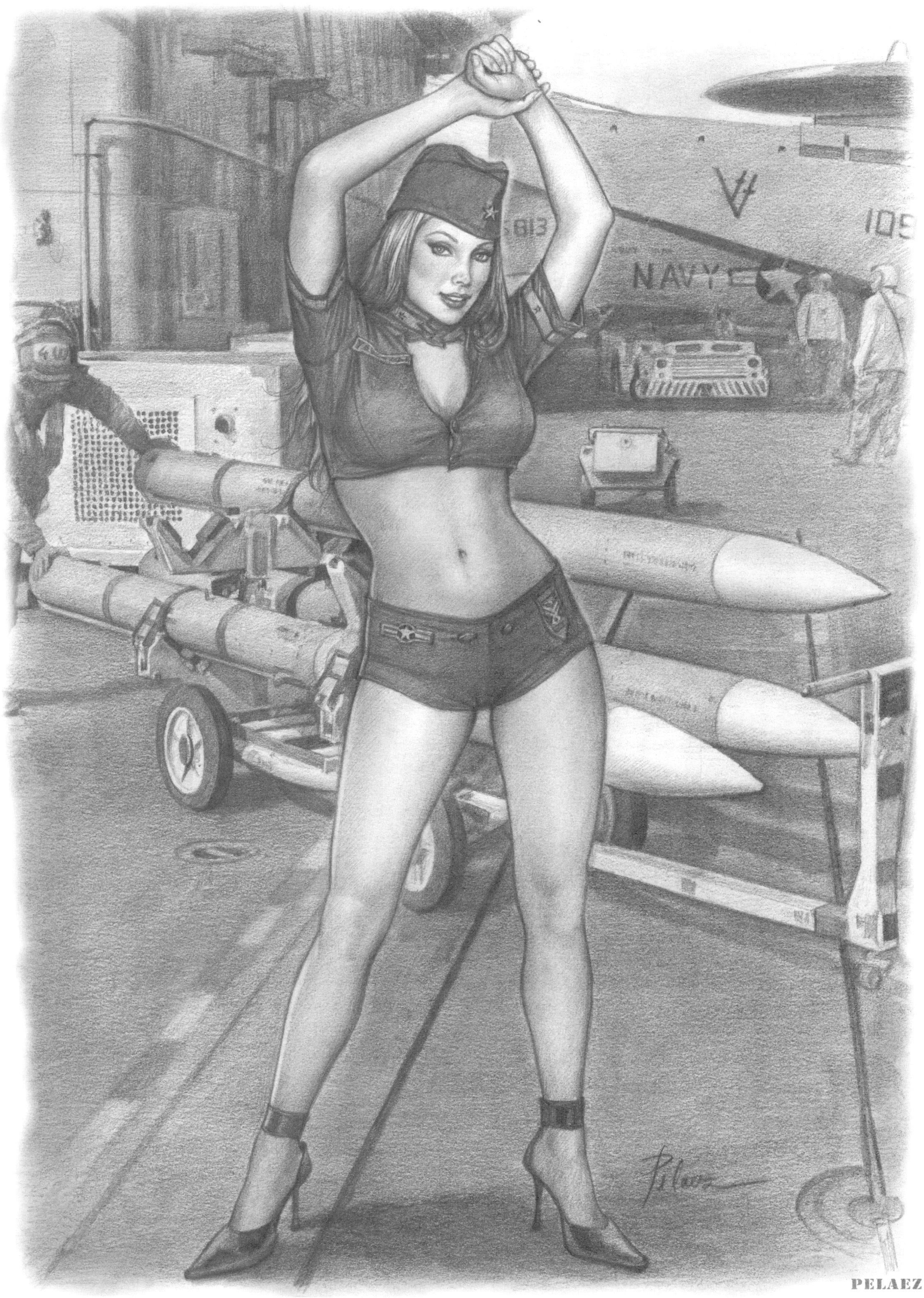

PELAEZ

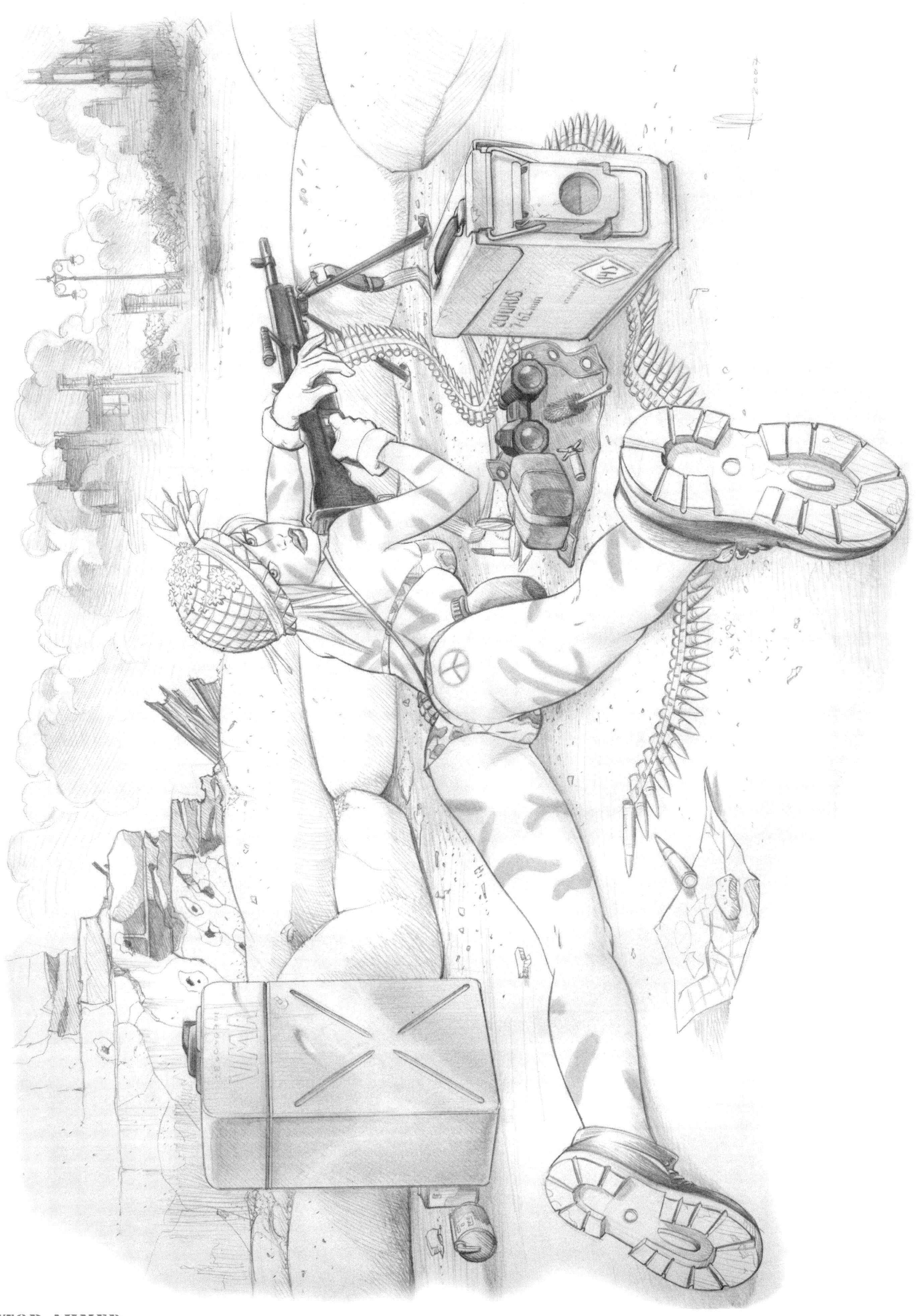

VICTOR AHMED

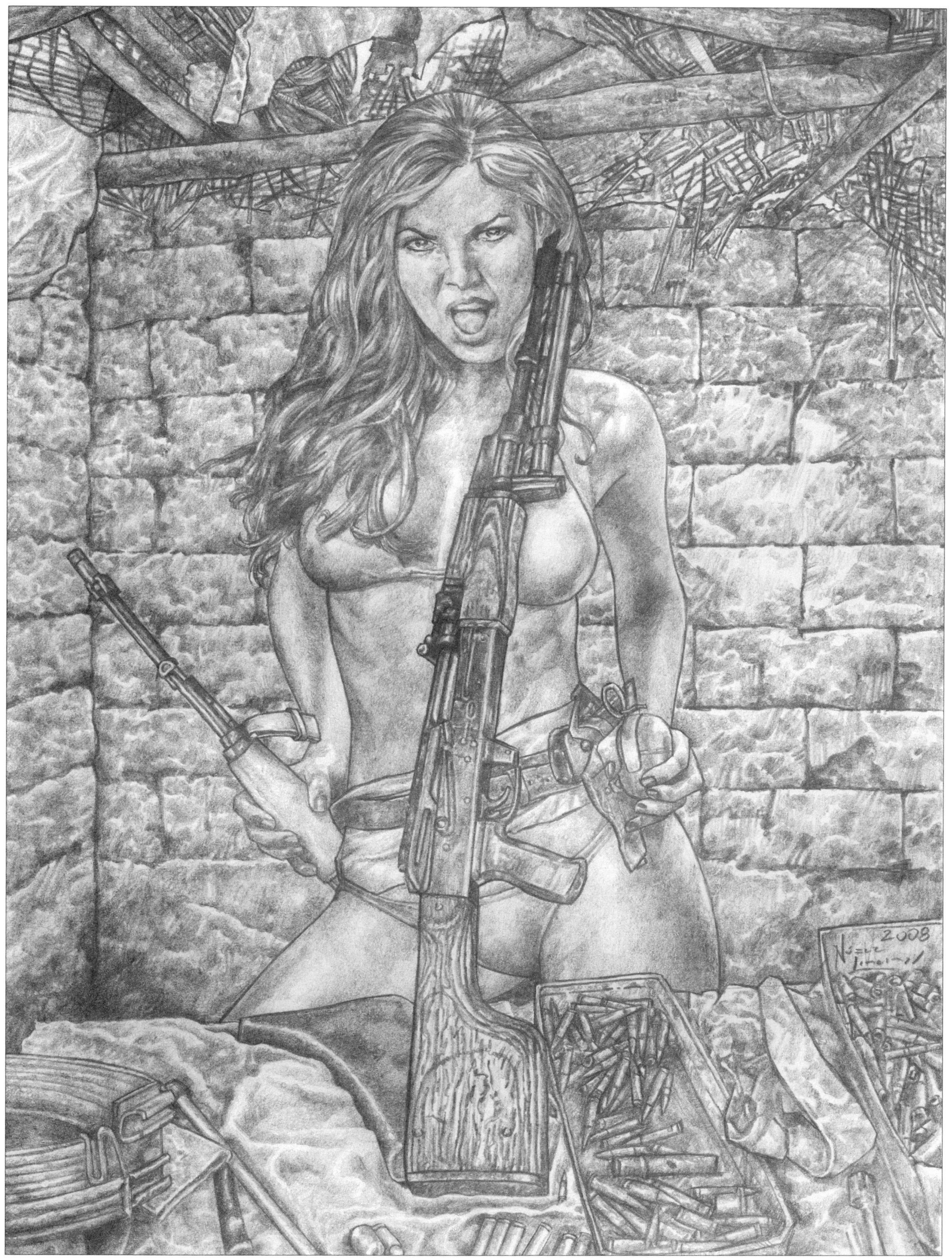

JUAN LENCINA

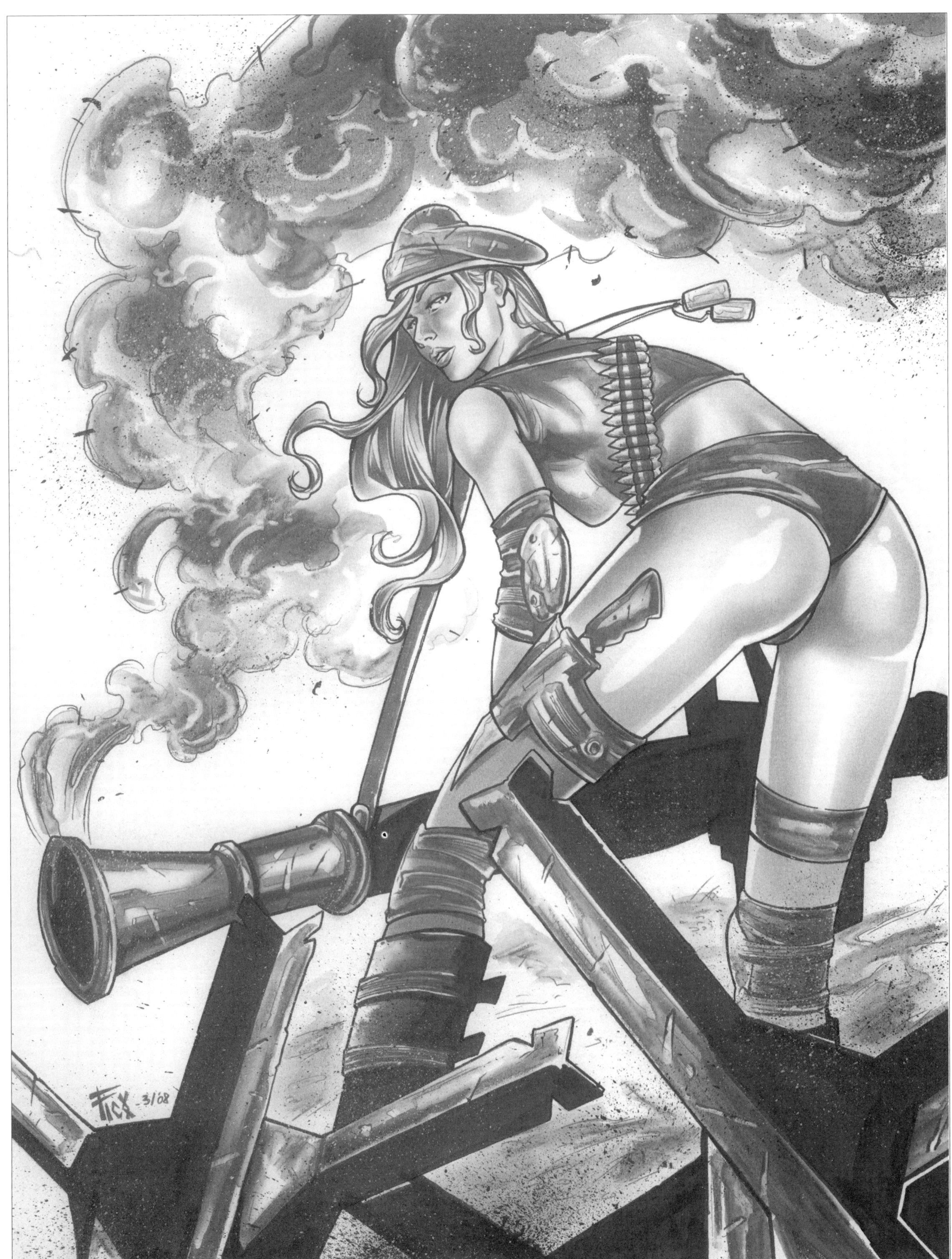

FEDERICO OSSIO

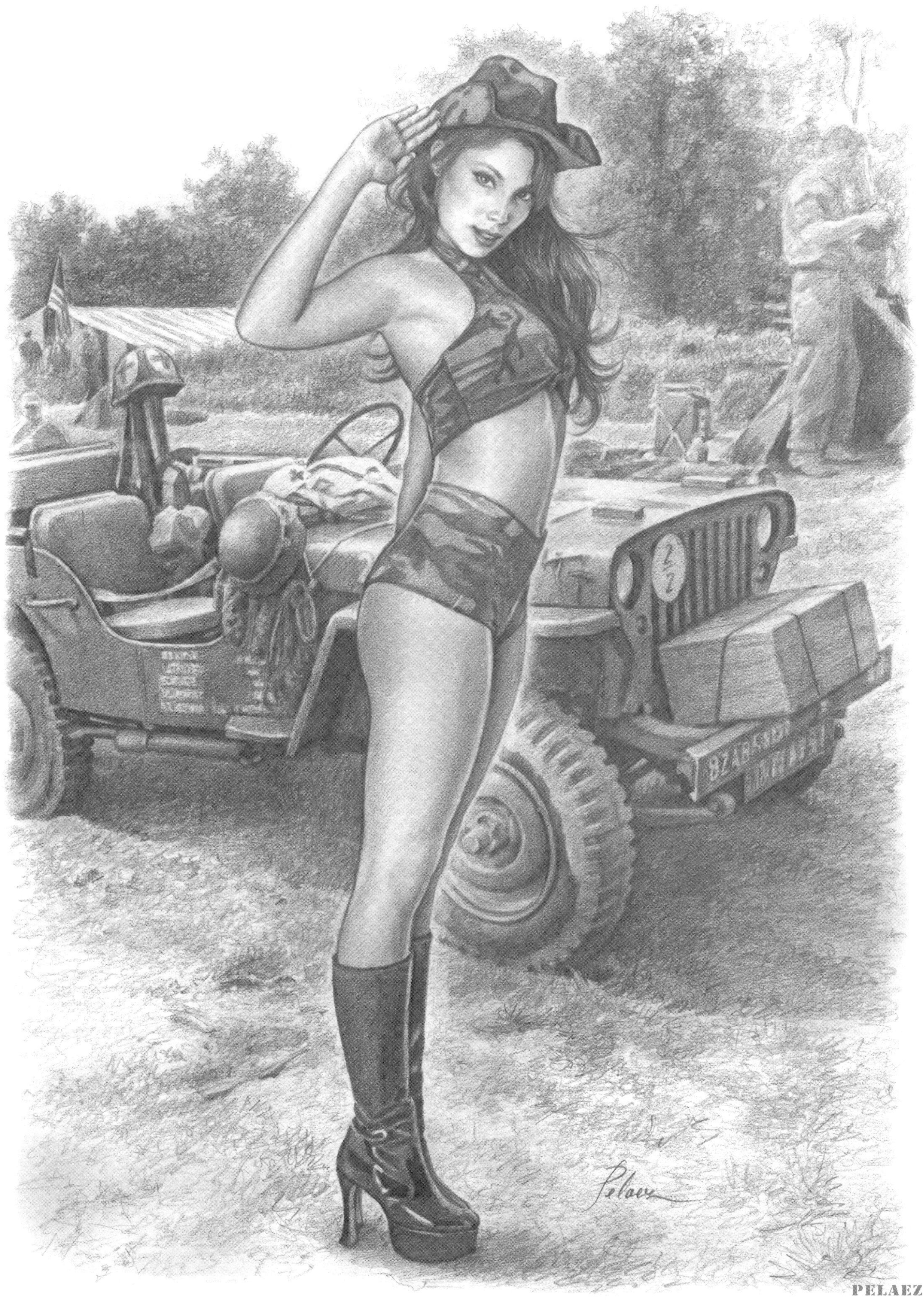

PELAEZ

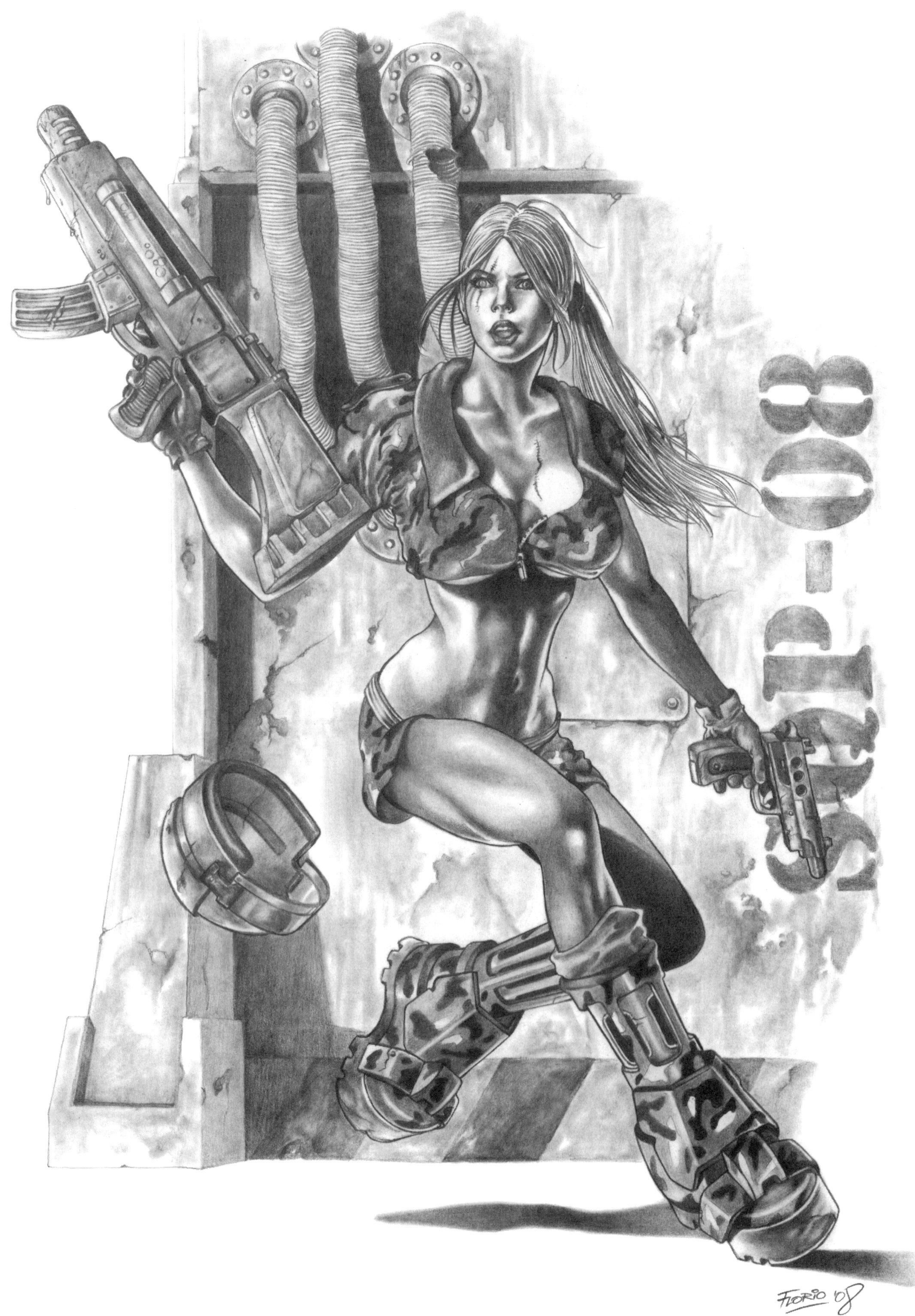

DIEGO FLORIO

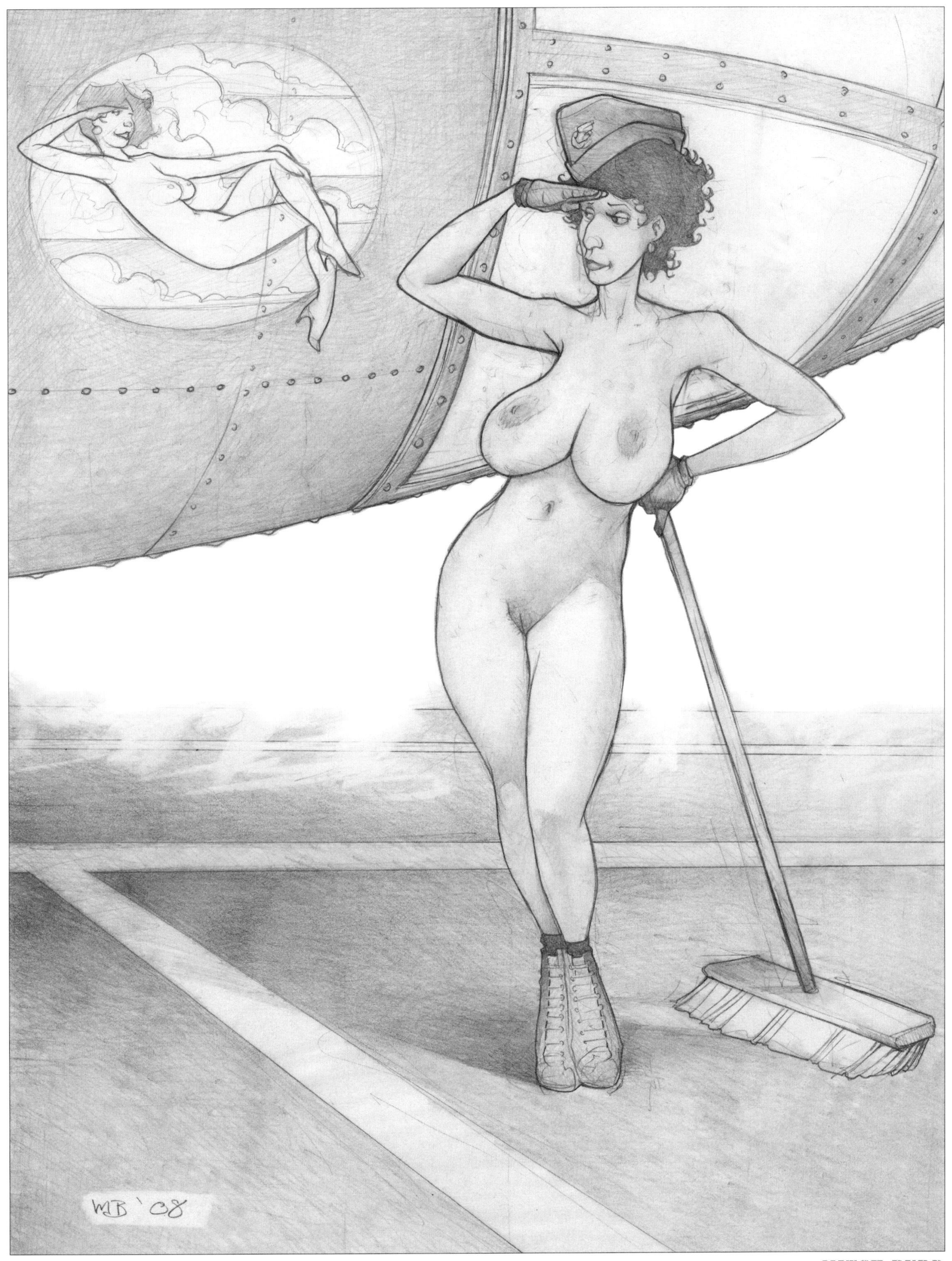

MITCH BYRD

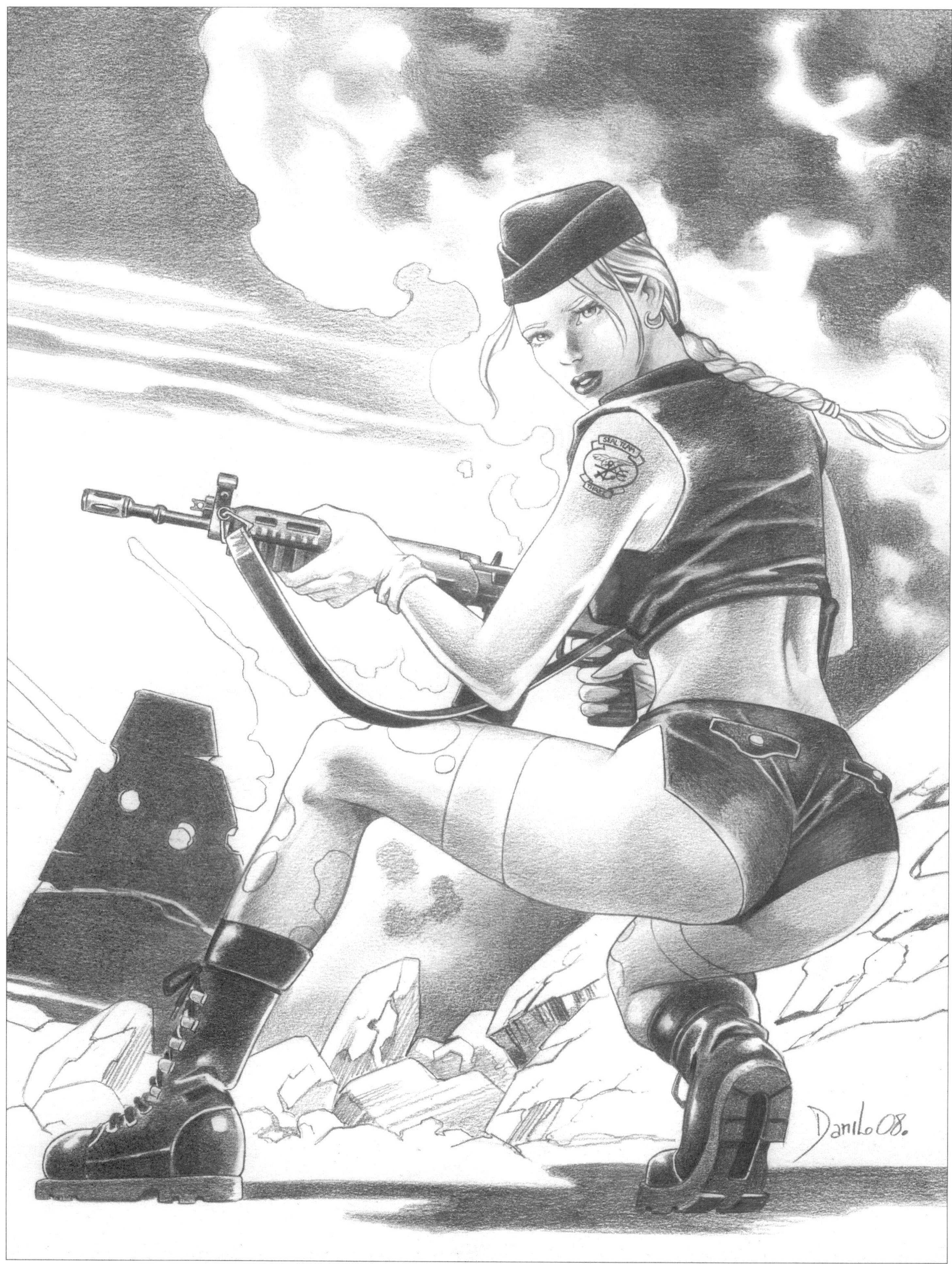

DANILO GUIDA

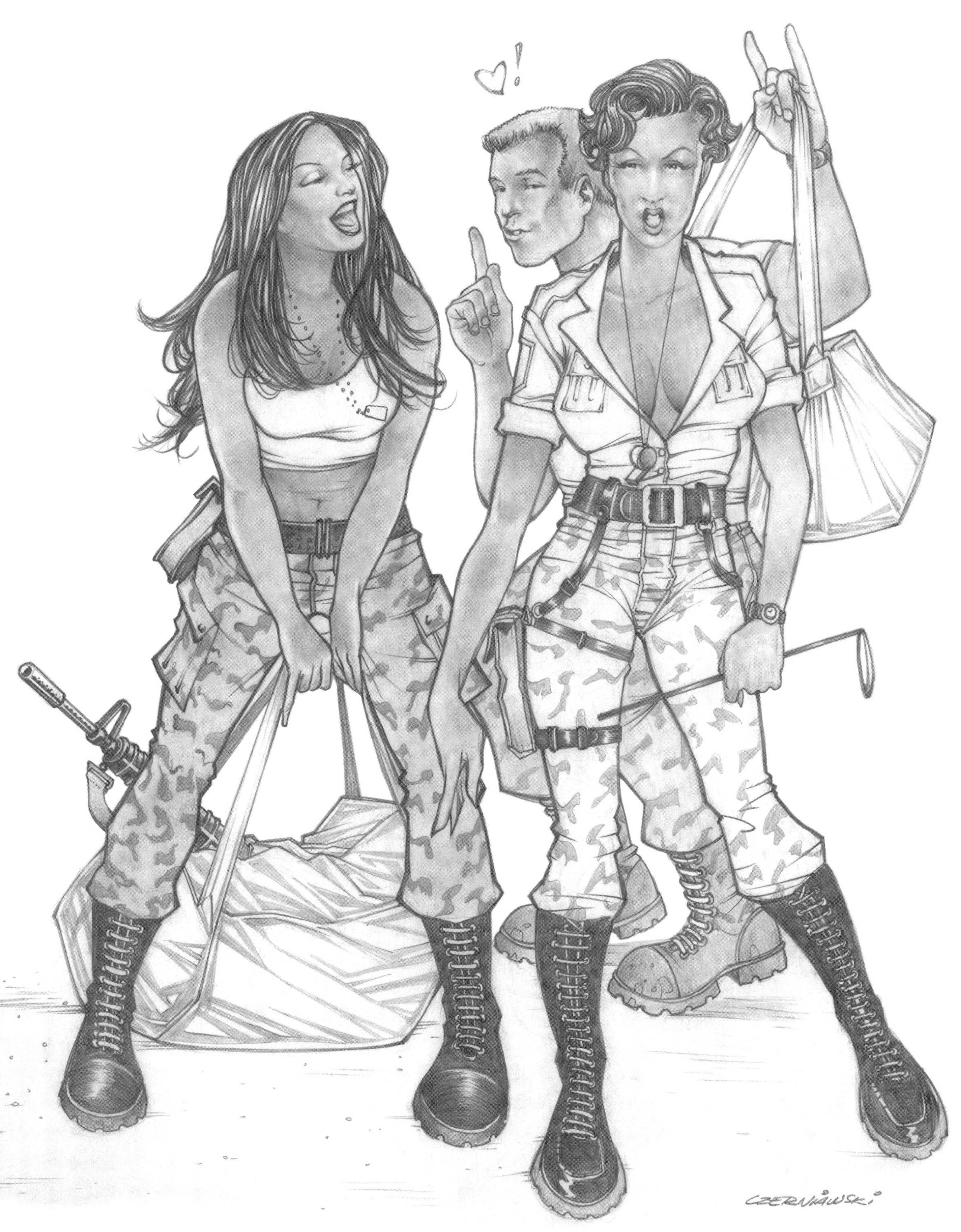

J.L. CZERNIAWSKI

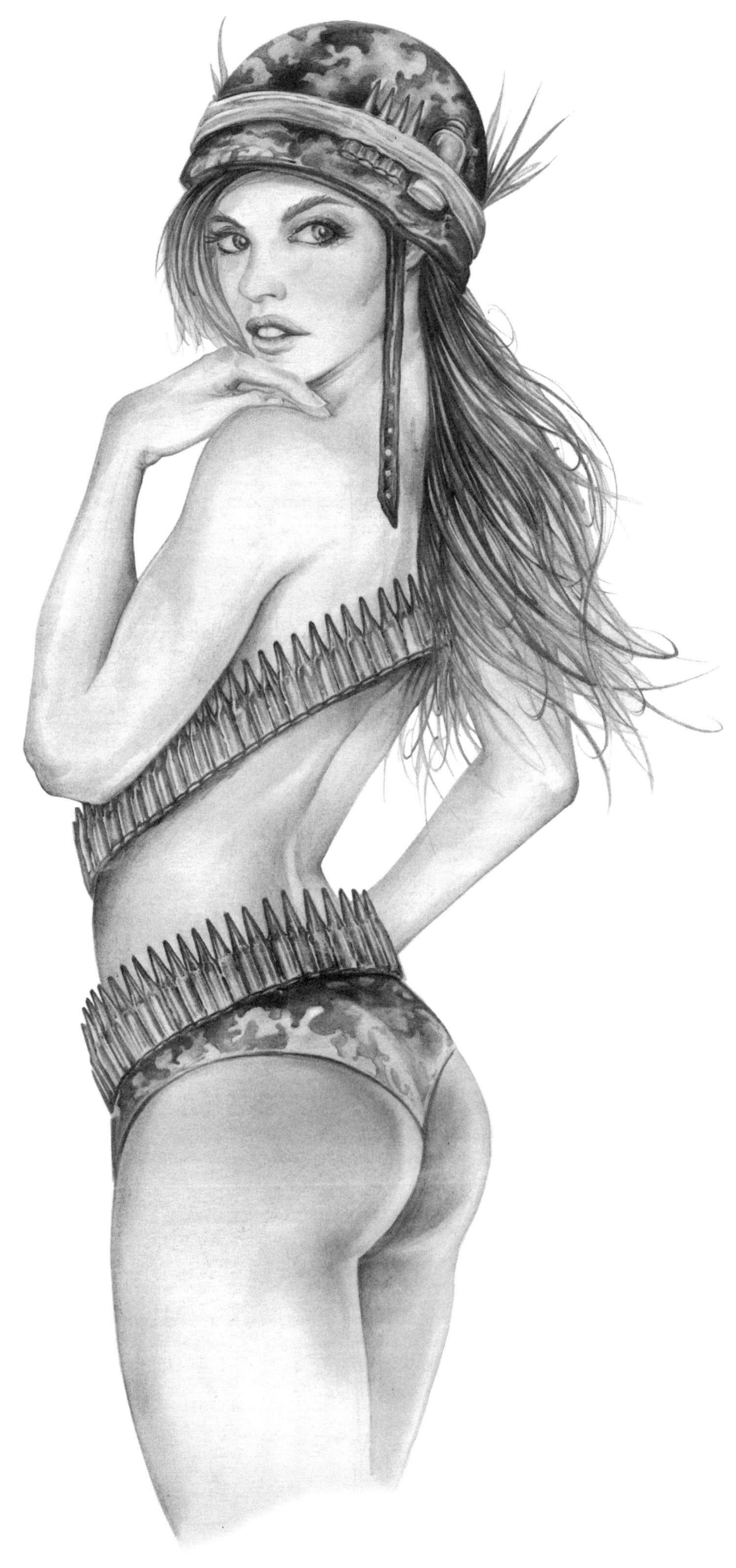

ALDO PEREZ

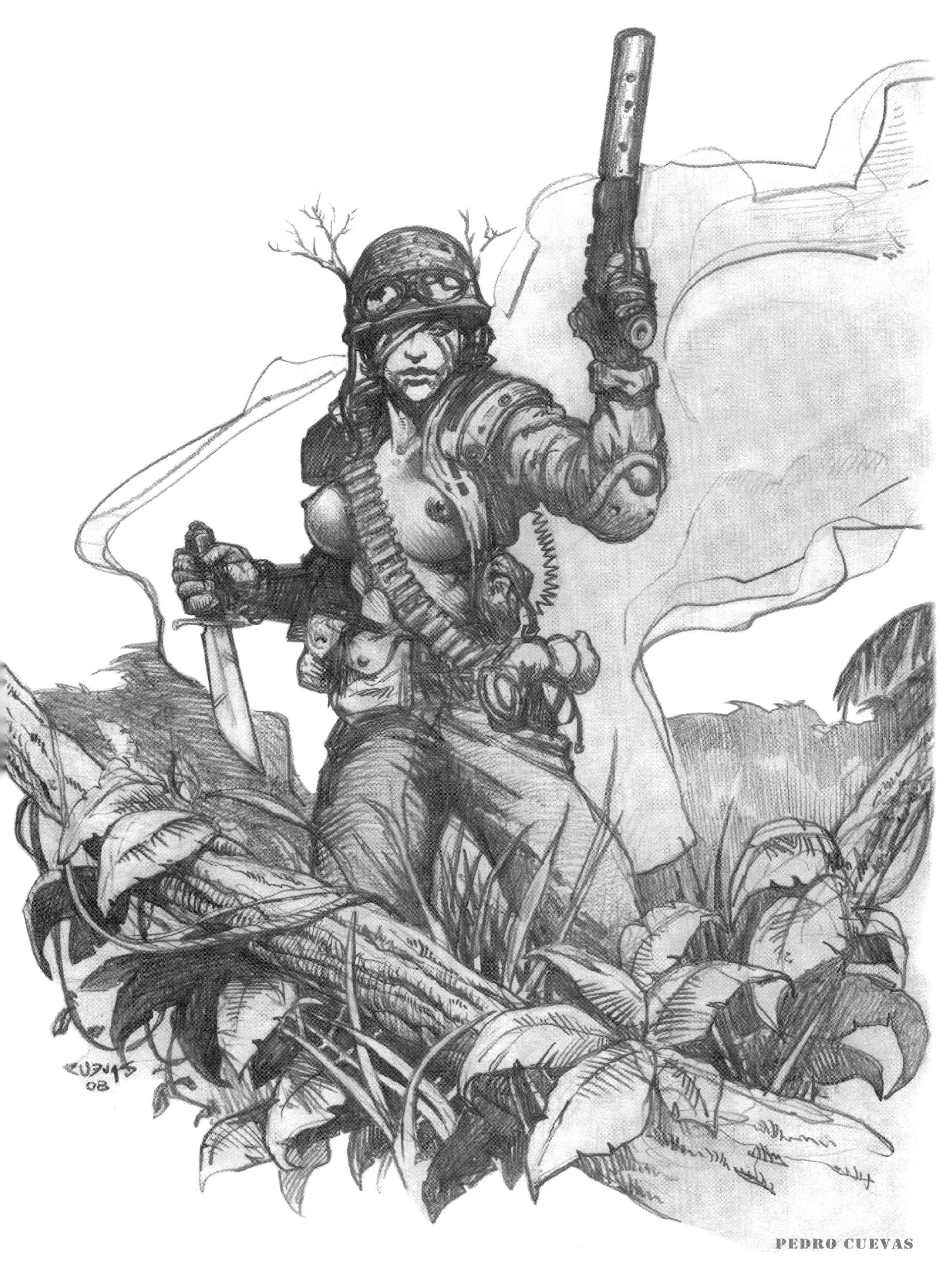

PEDRO CUEVAS

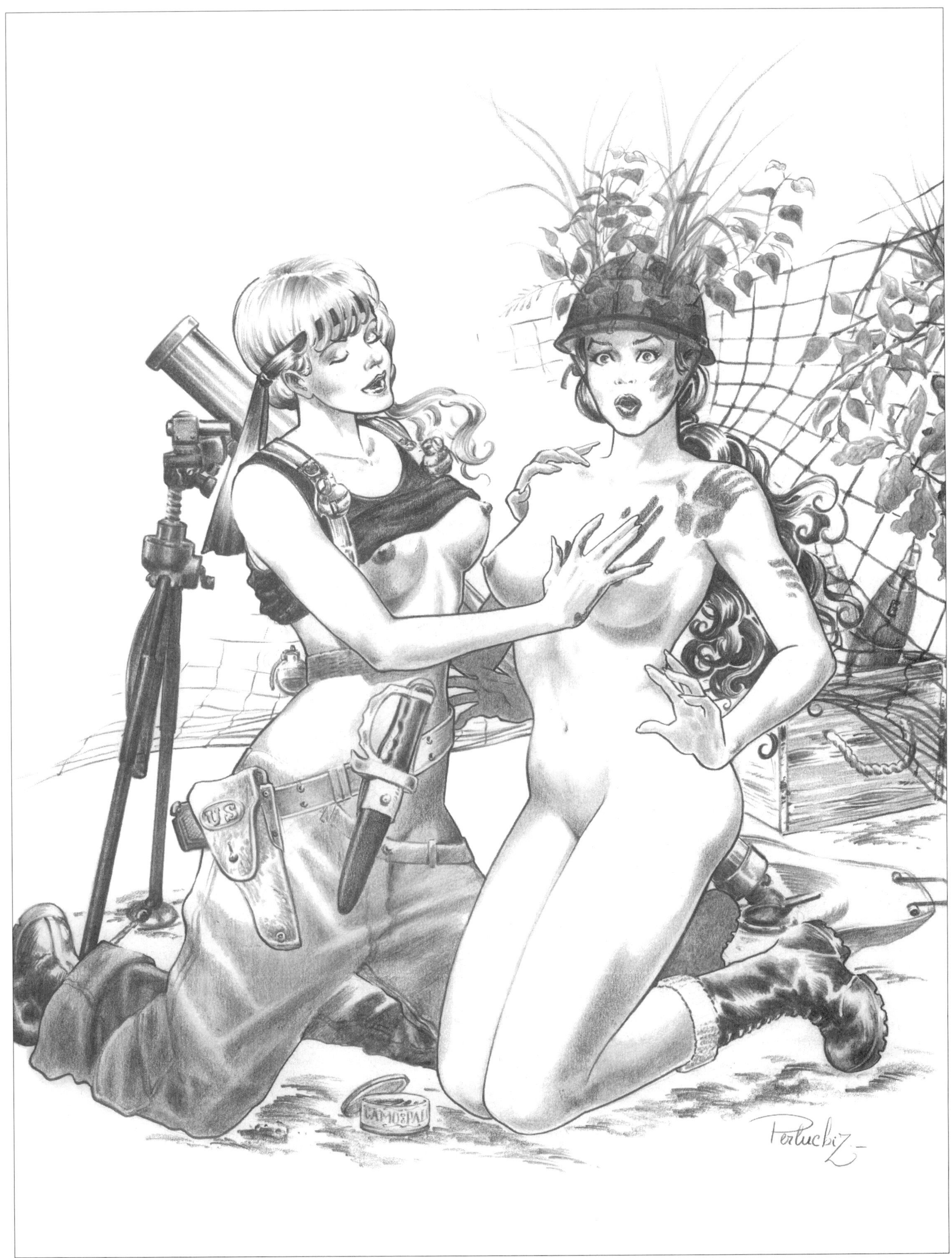

PERLA PILUCKI

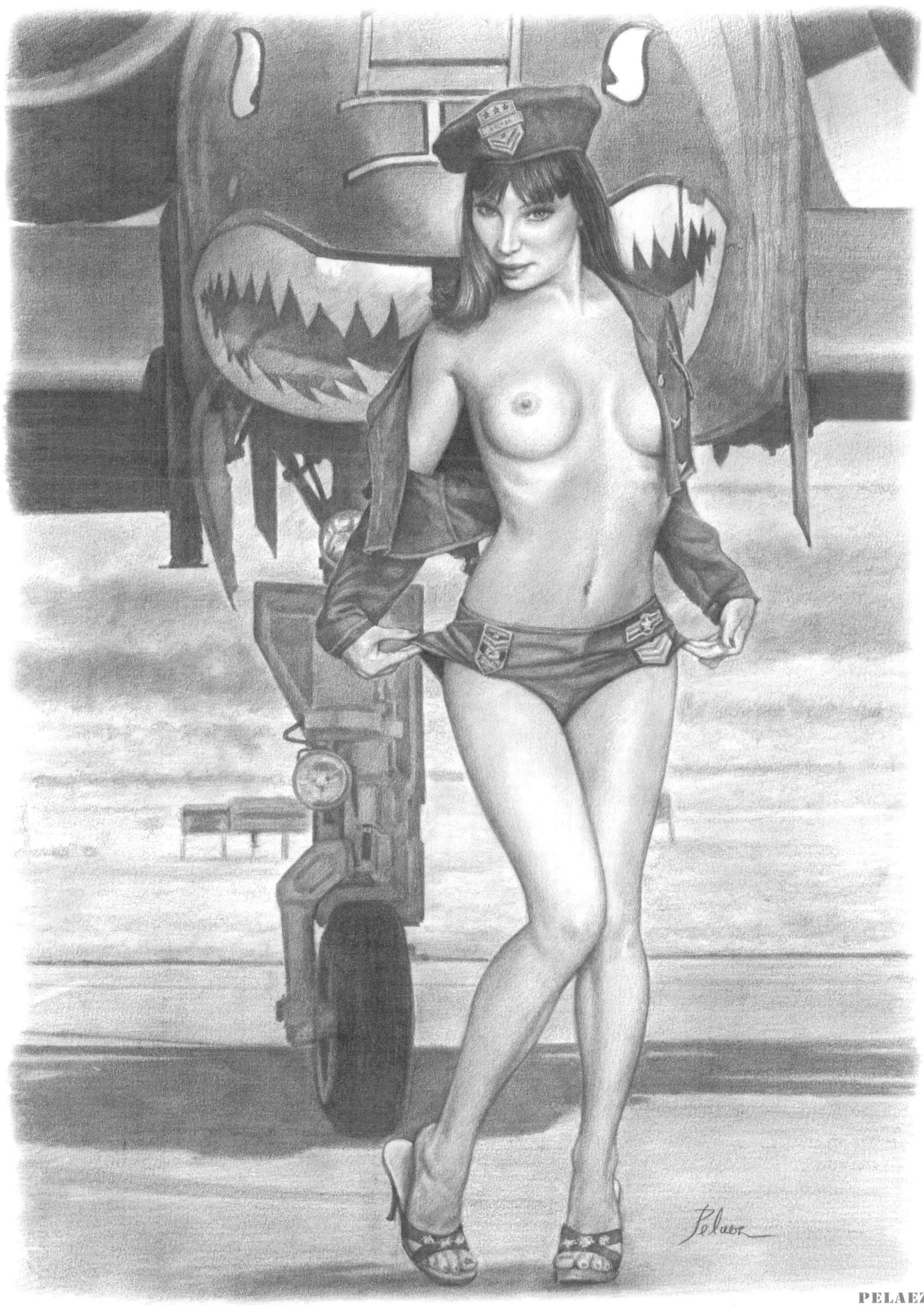

PELAEZ

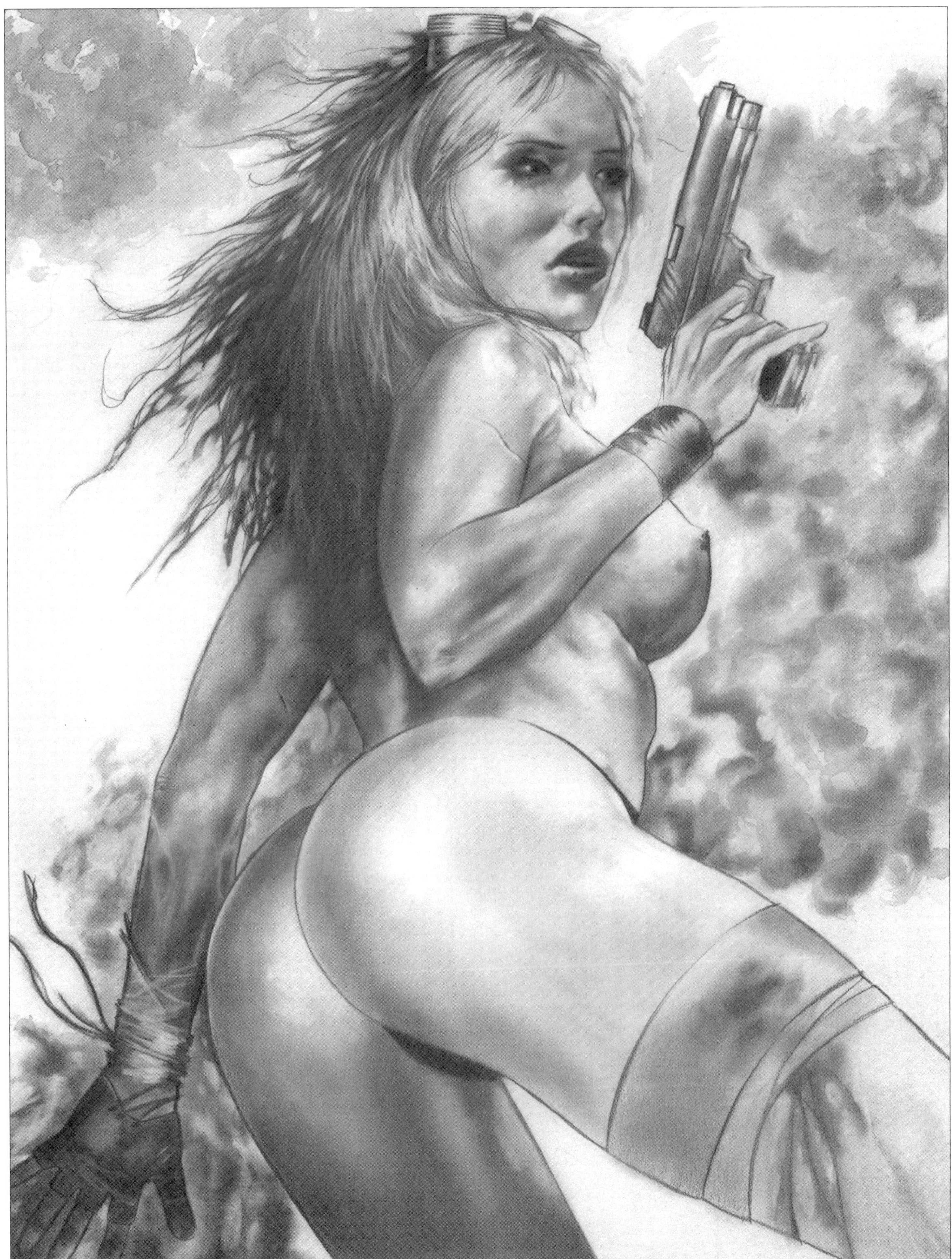

LUIS BUCI

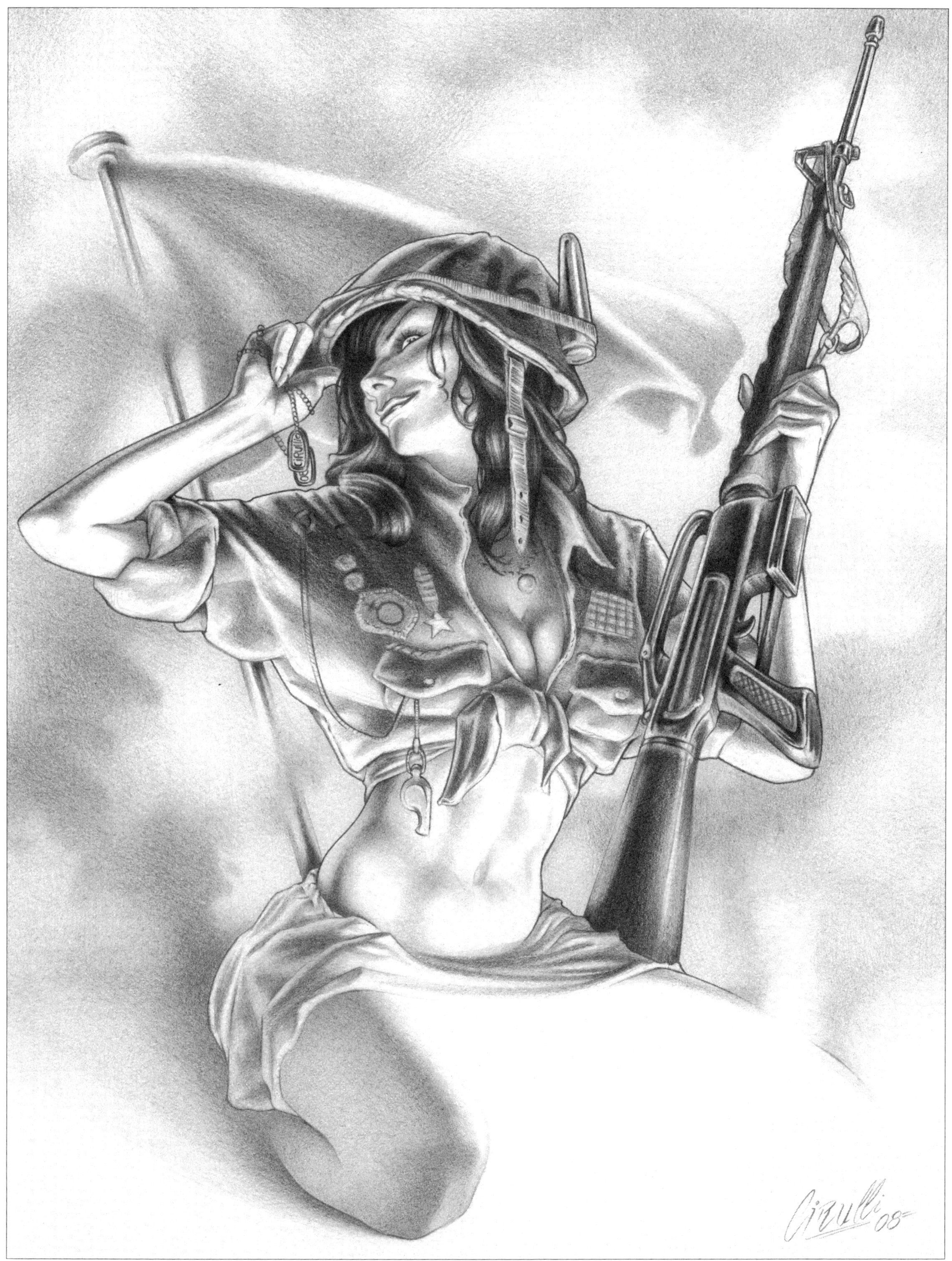

DIEGO CIRULLI

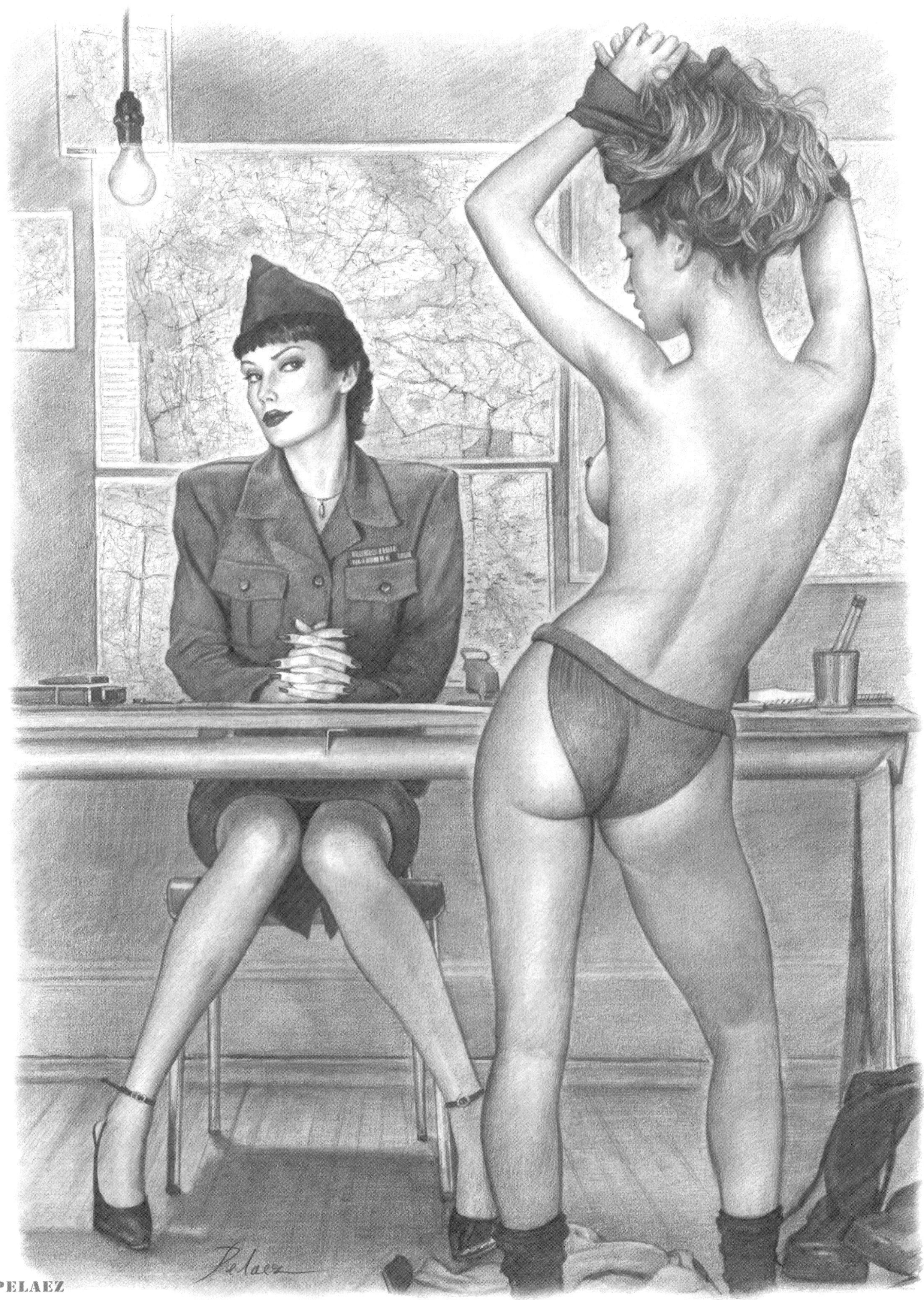

PELAEZ

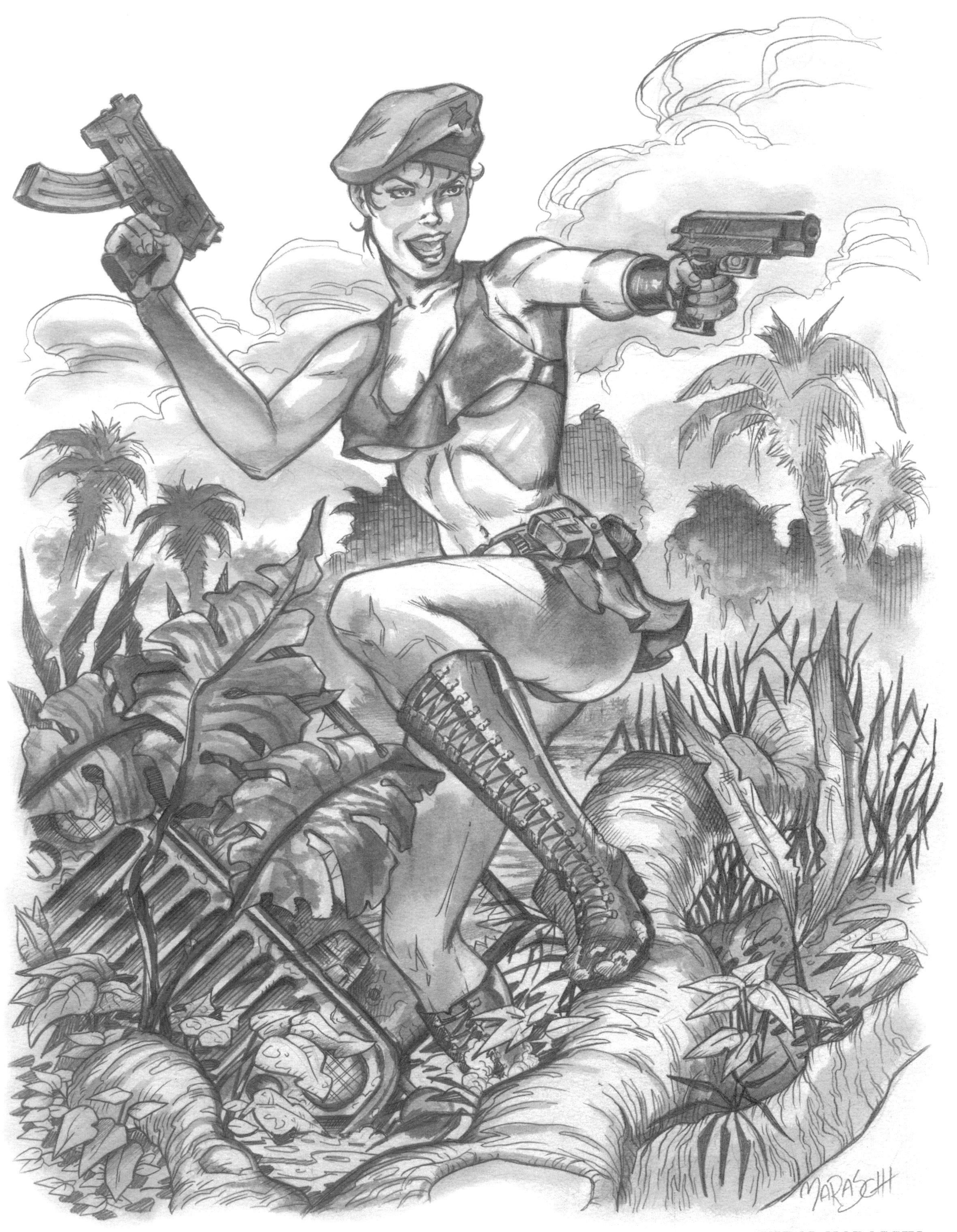

ANIBAL MARASCHI

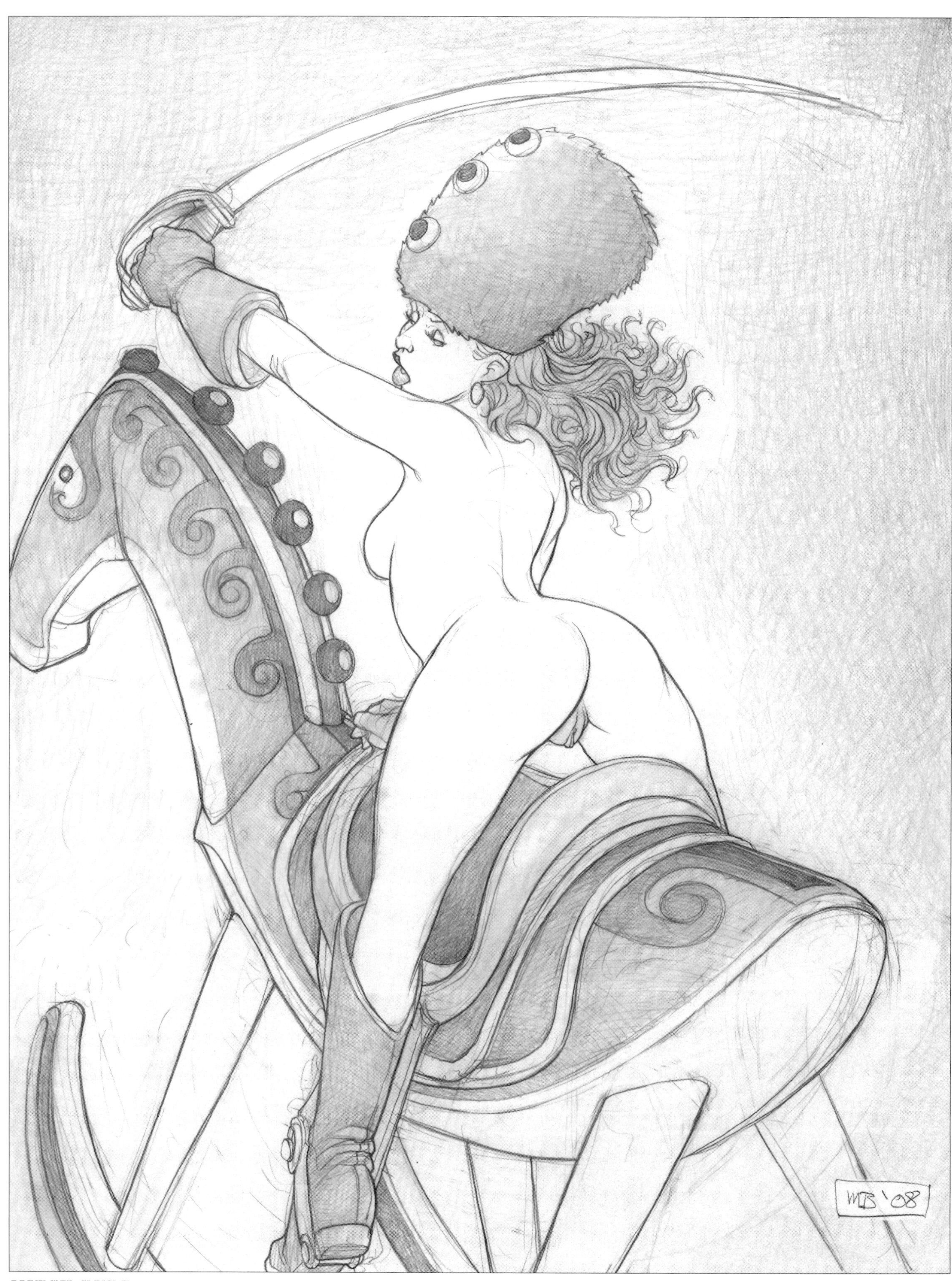

MITCH BYRD

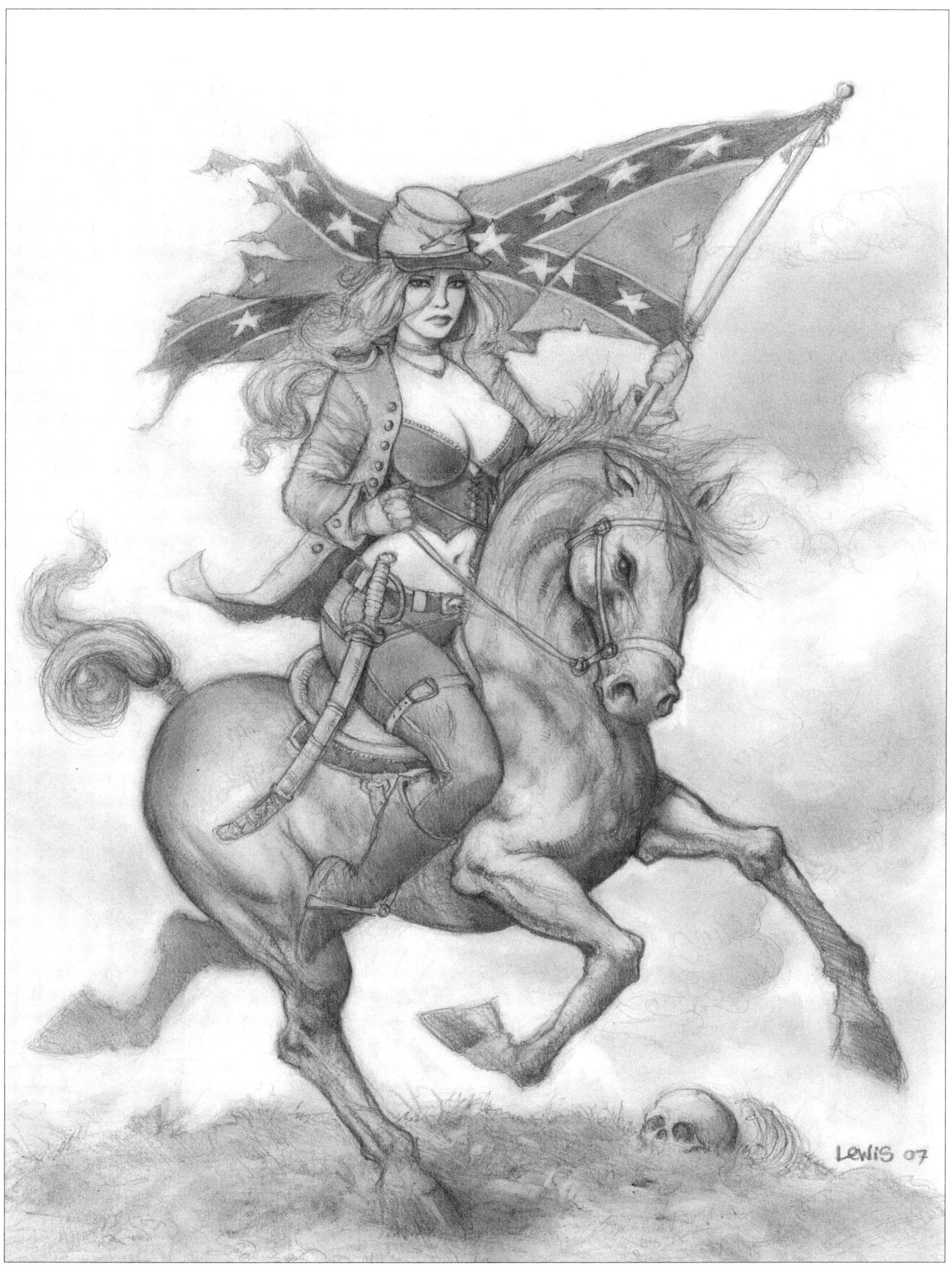

SCOTT LEWIS

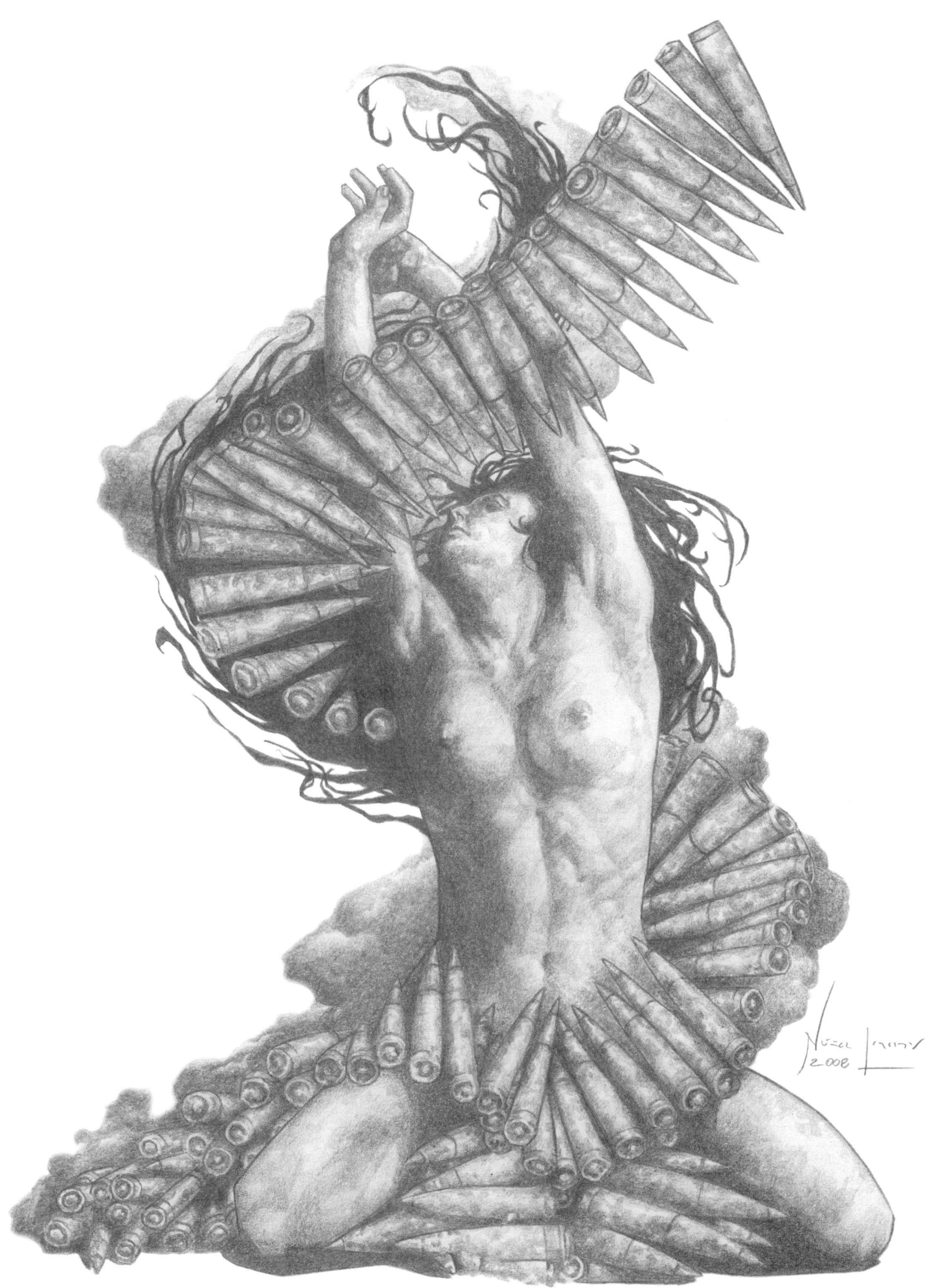

JUAN LENCINA

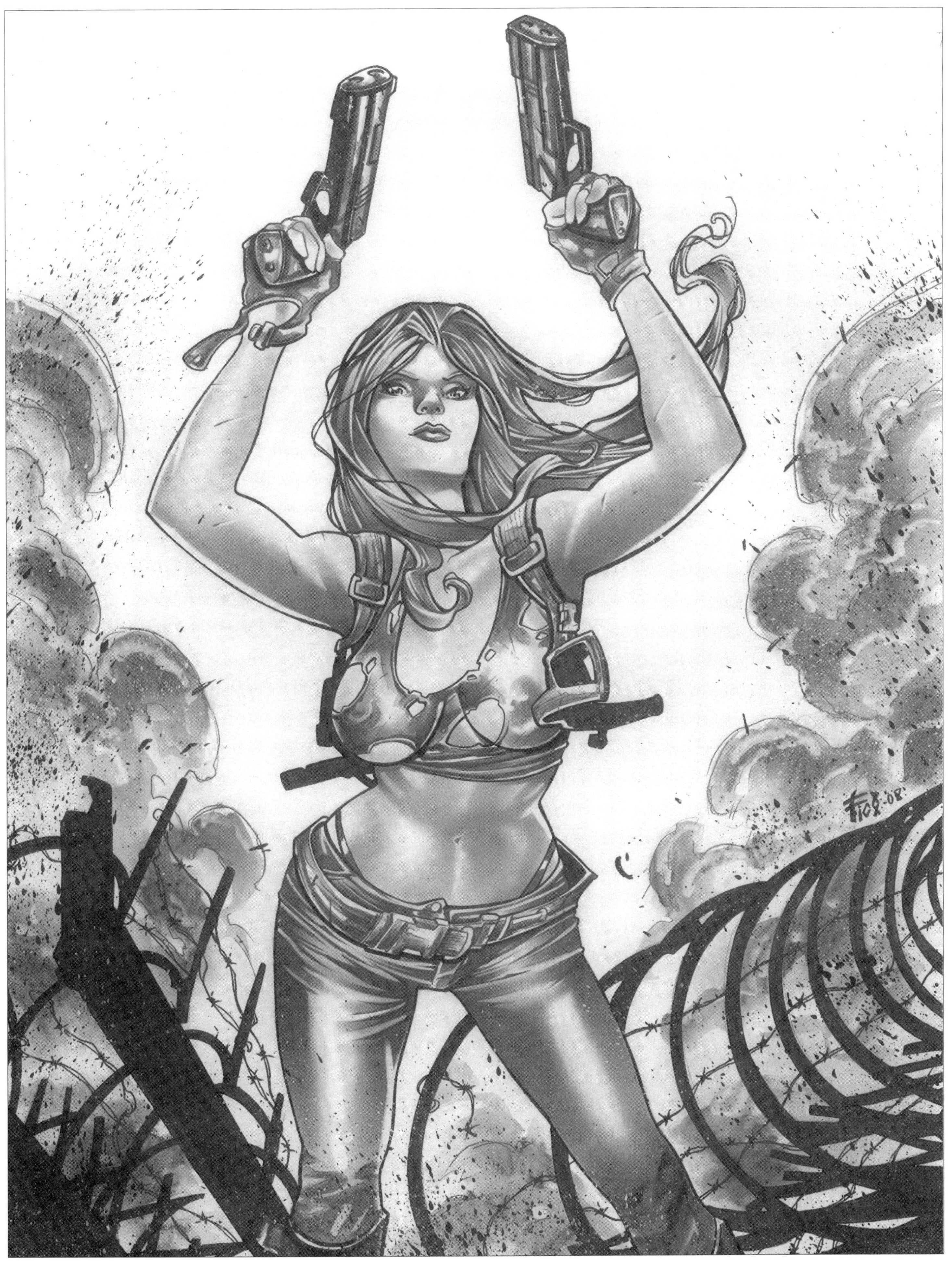

FEDERICO OSSIO

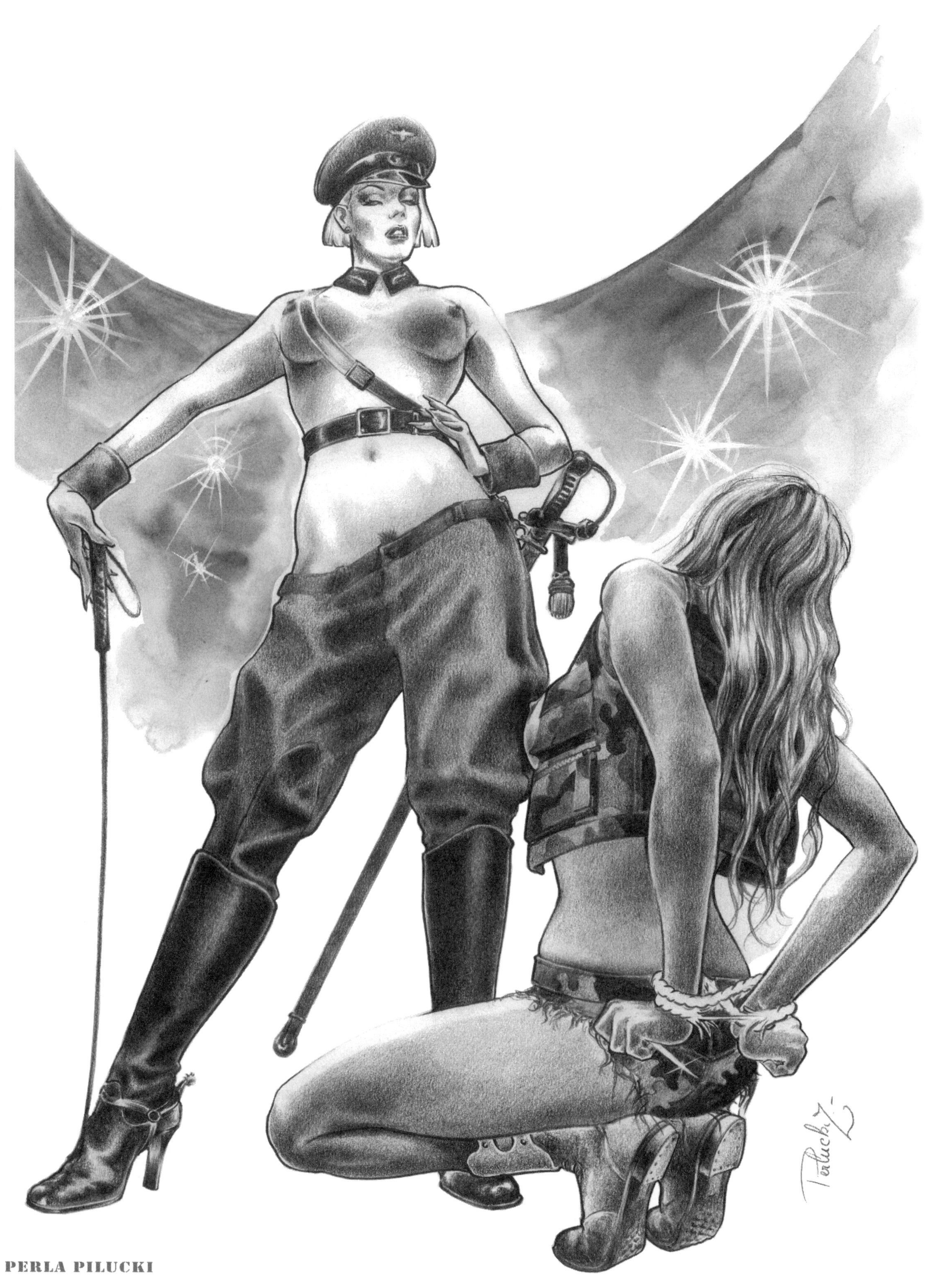

PERLA PILUCKI

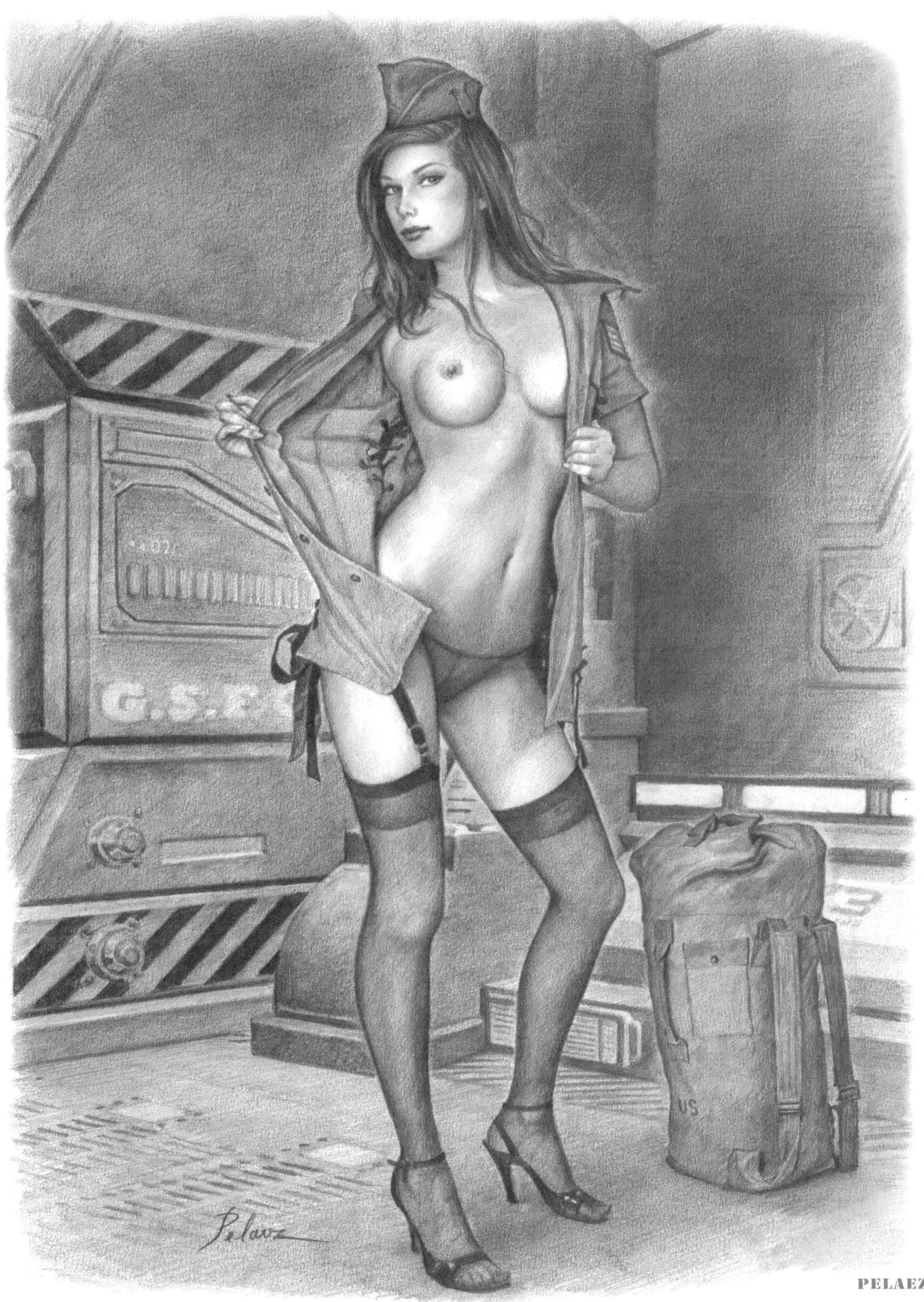

PELAEZ

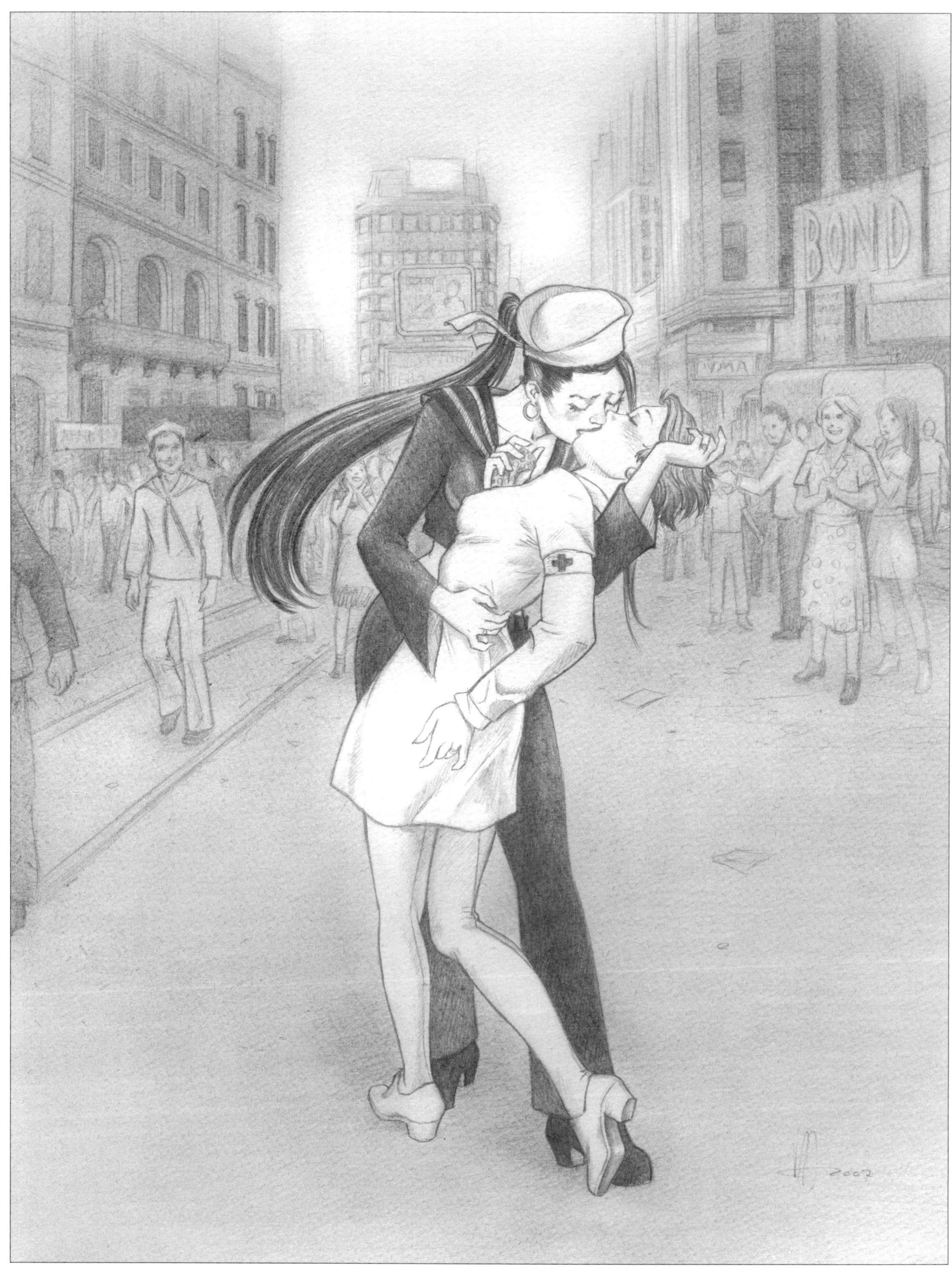

VICTOR AHMED

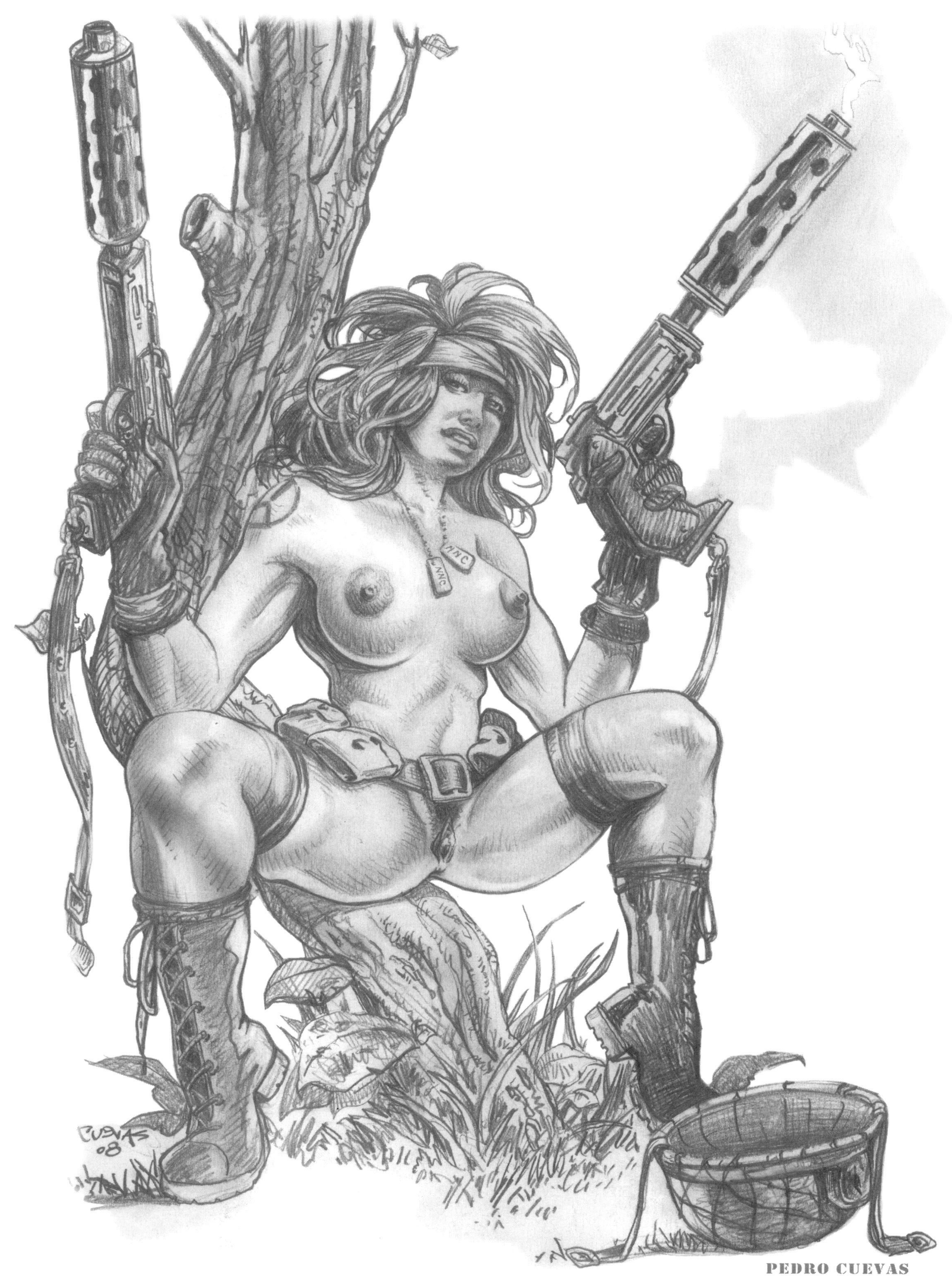

PEDRO CUEVAS

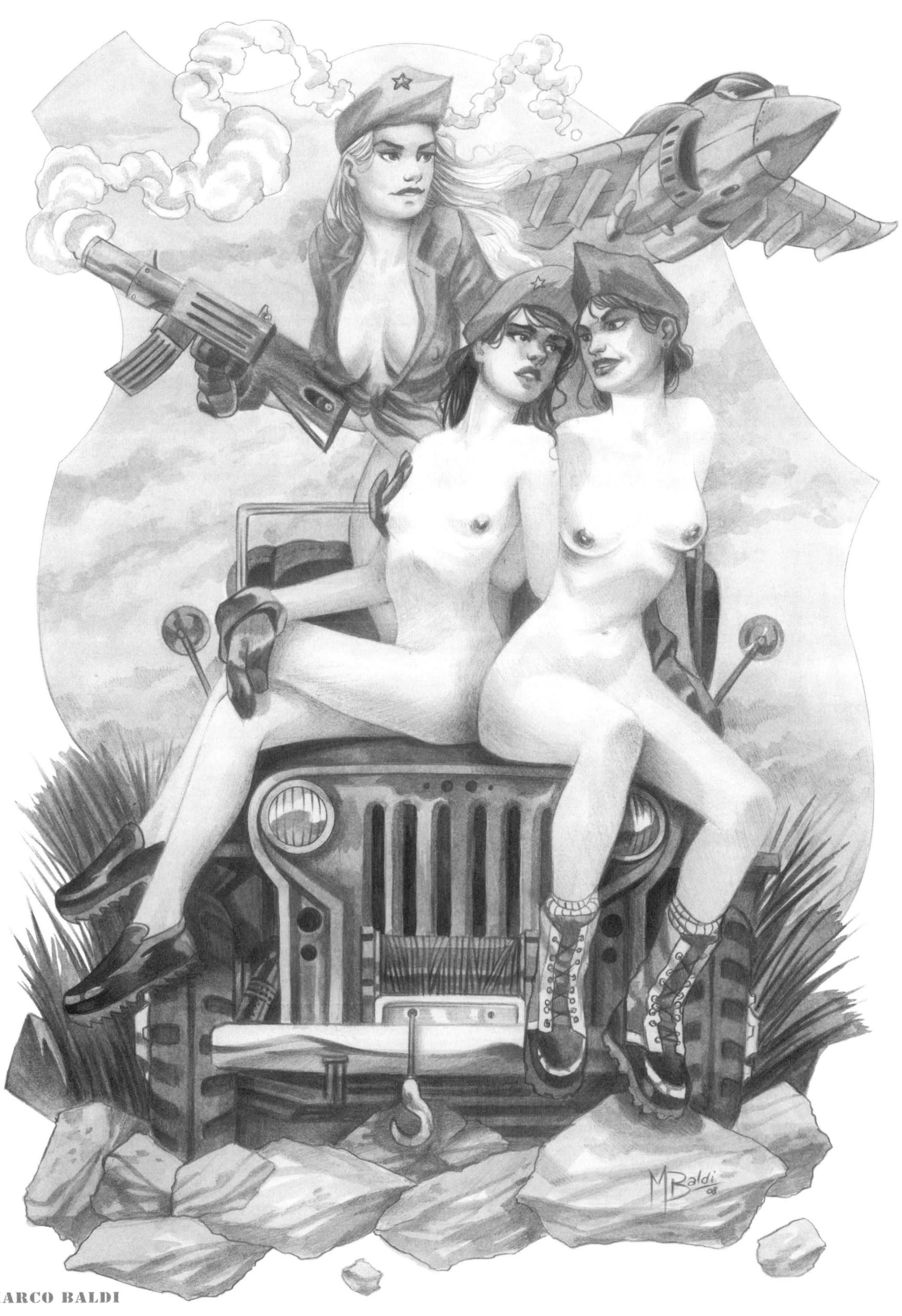

MARCO BALDI

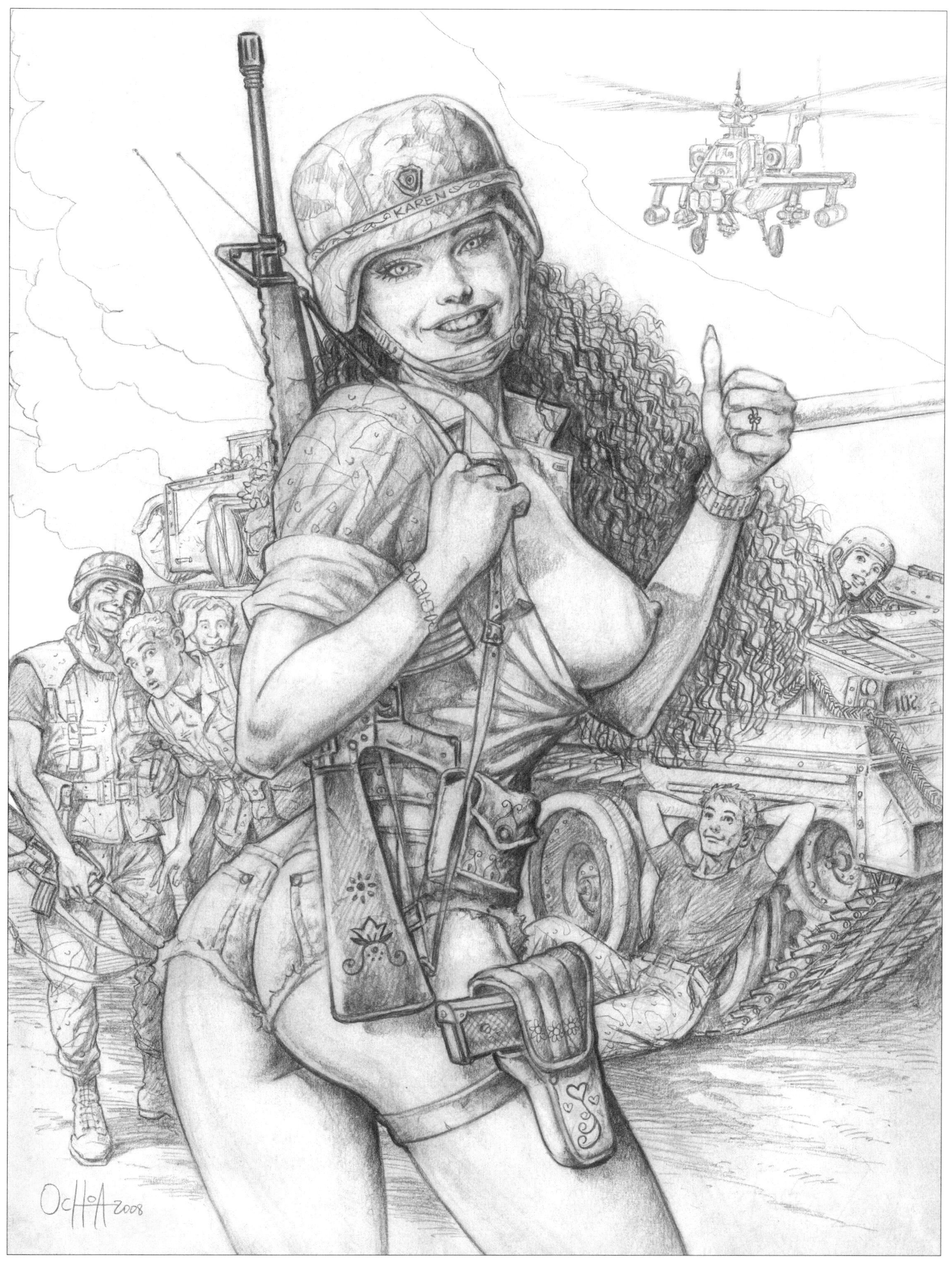

PERCY OCHOA

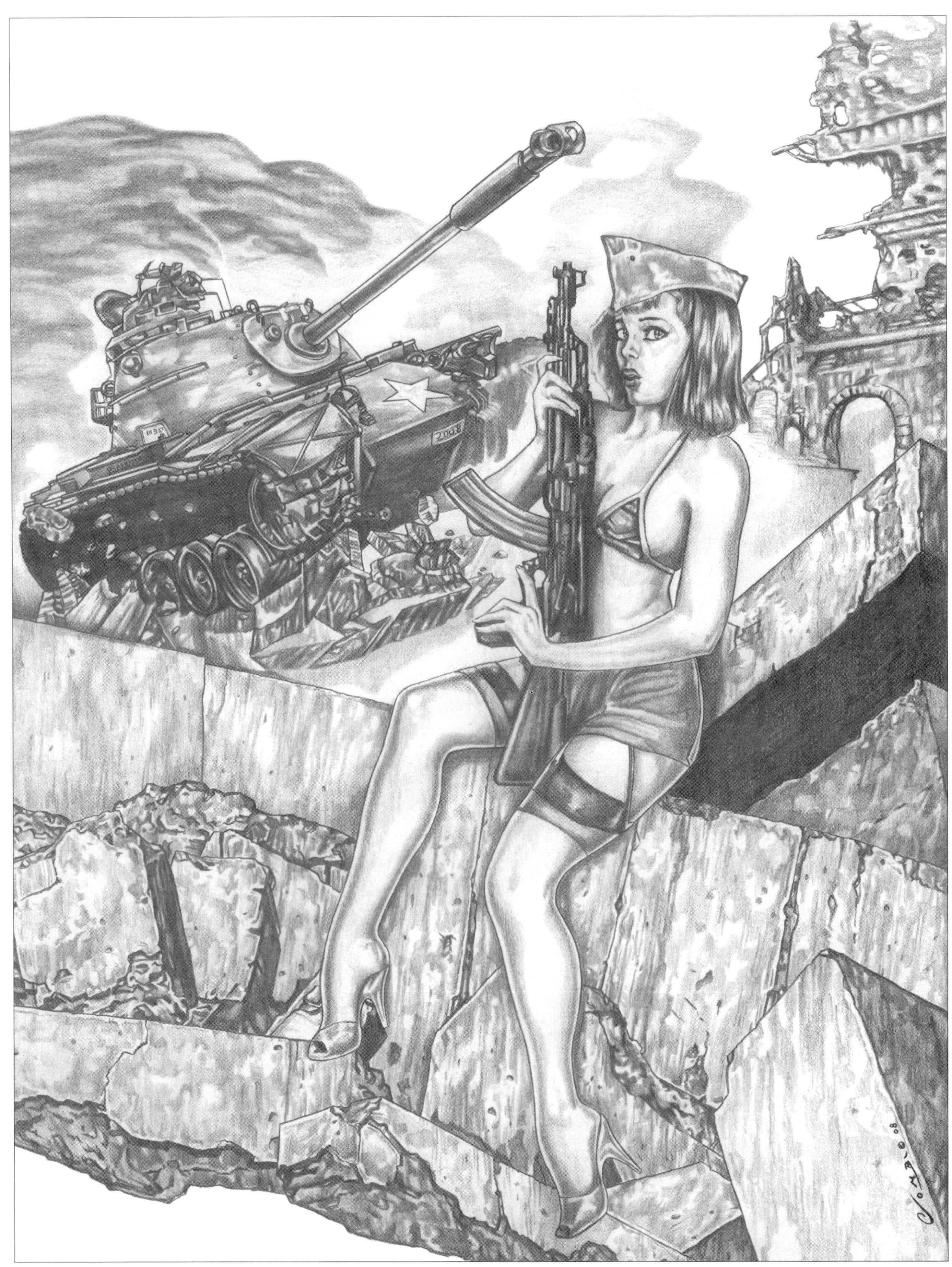

FEDERICO COMBI

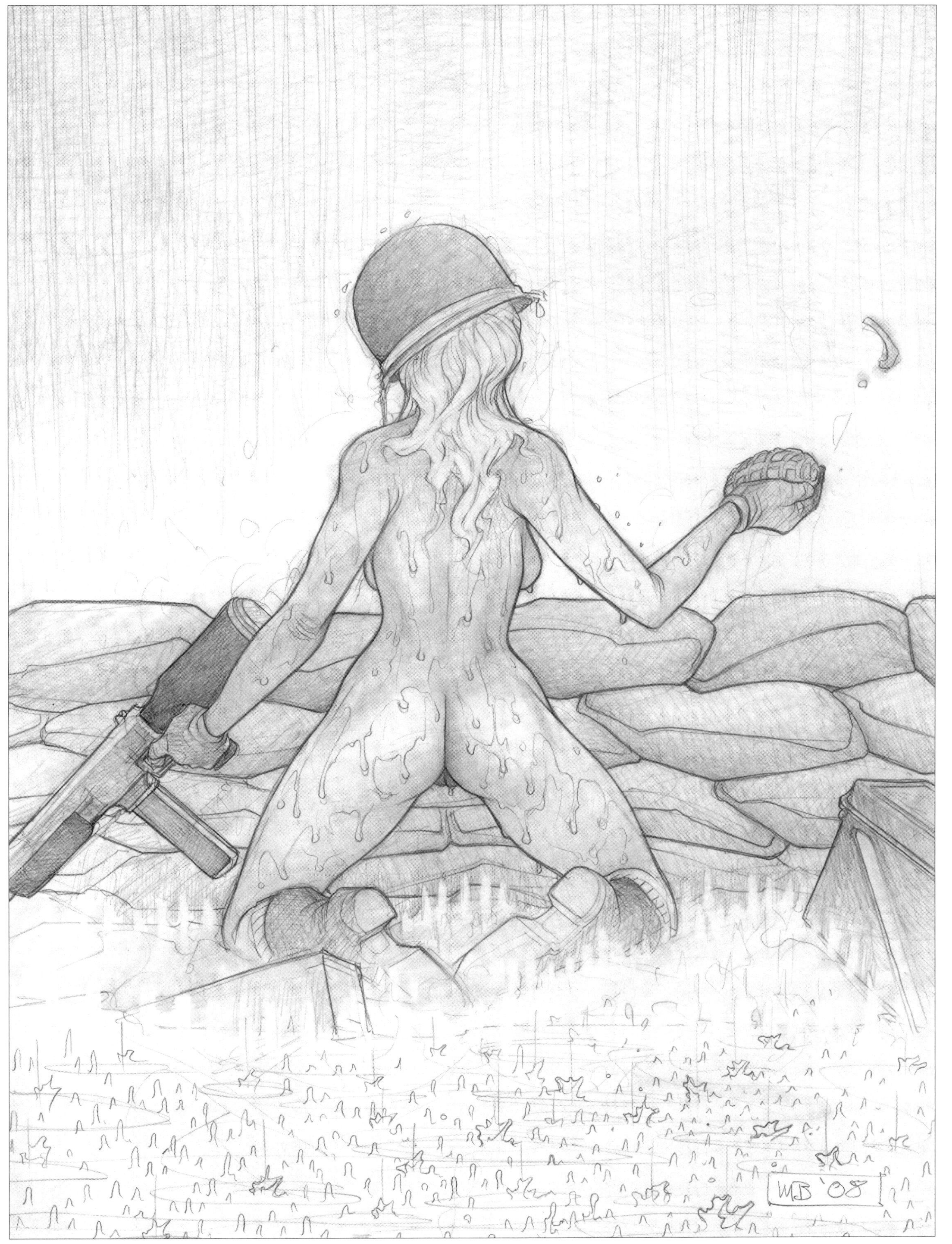

MITCH BYRD

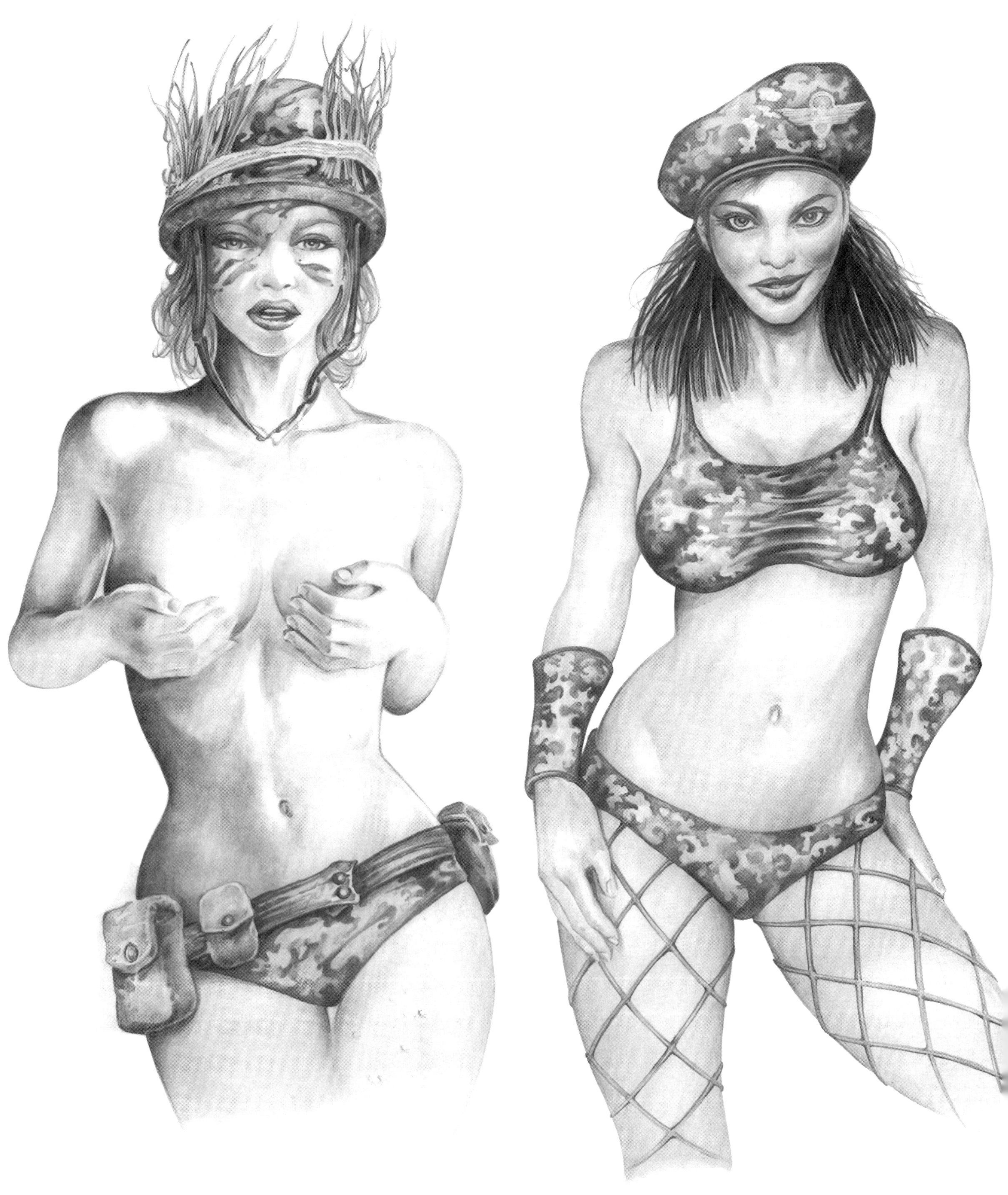

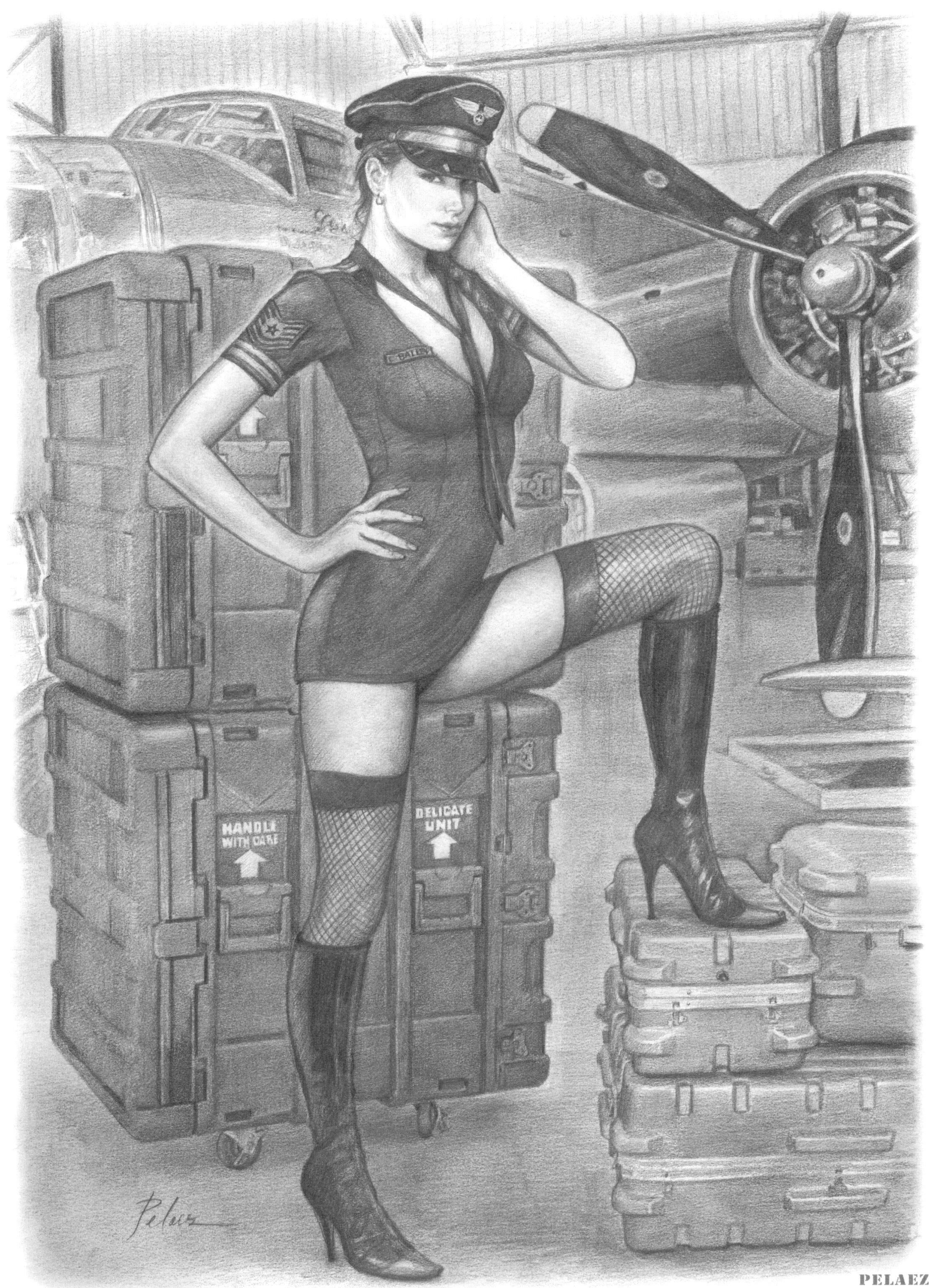

PELAEZ

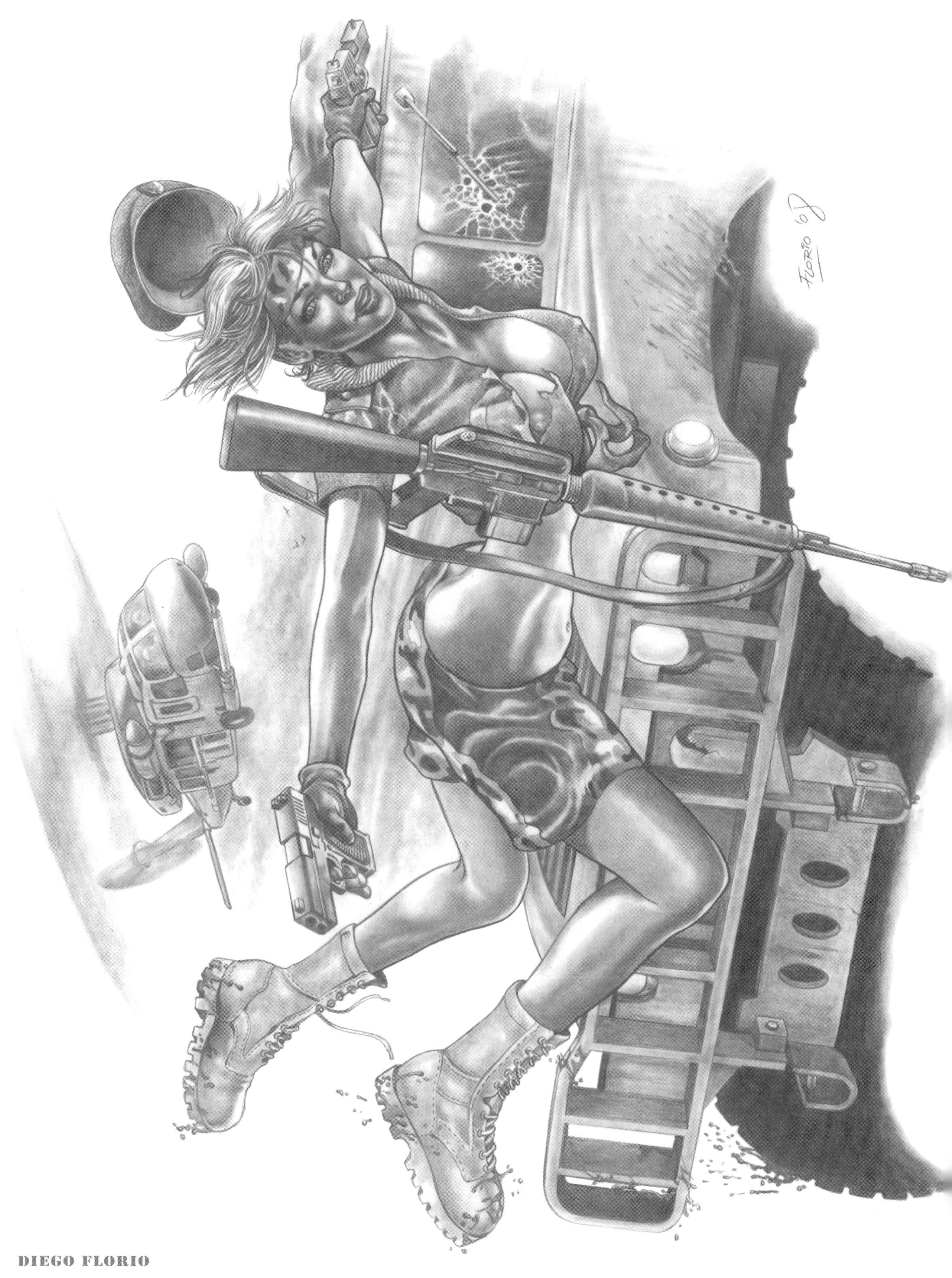

DIEGO FLORIO

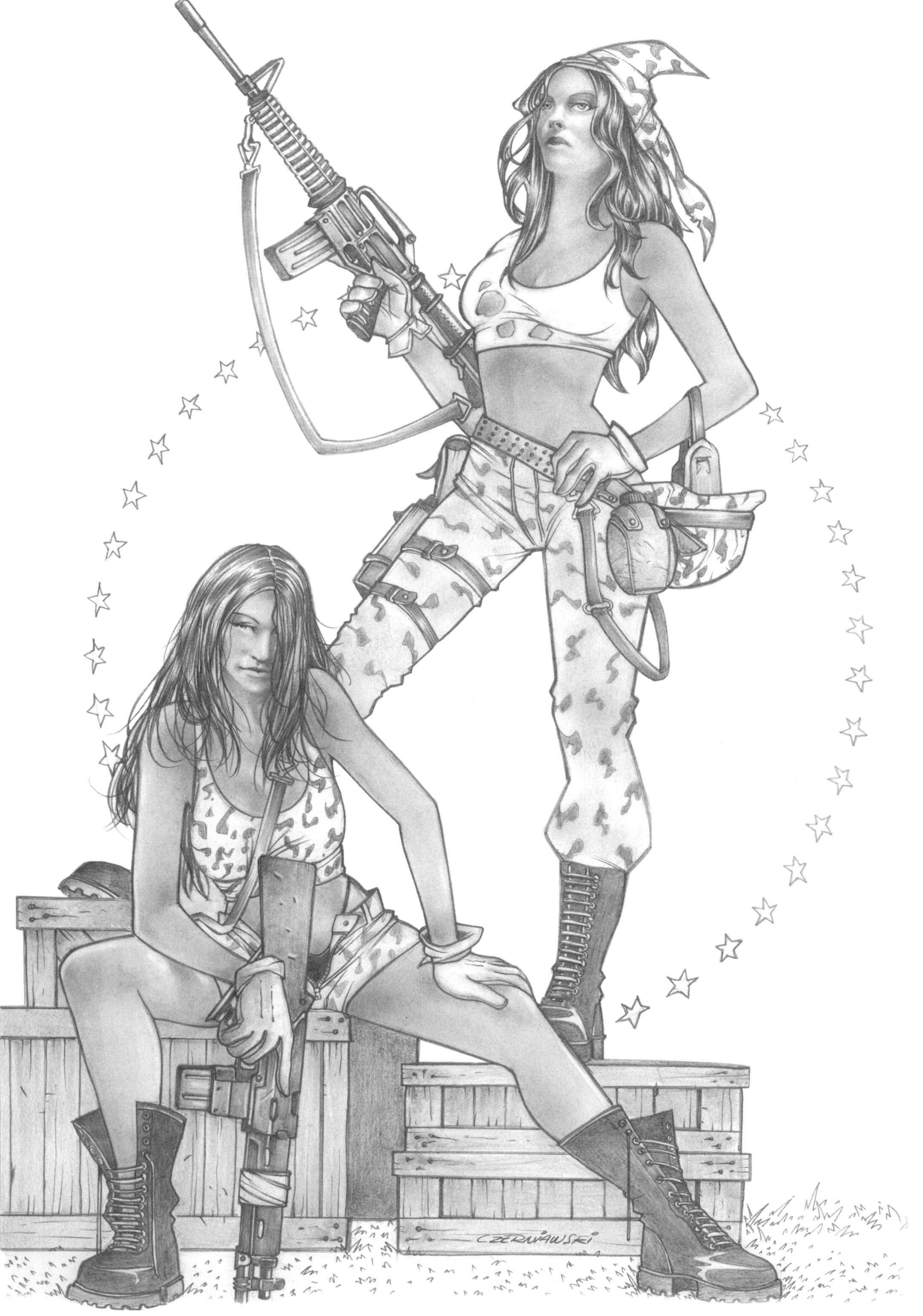

J.L. CZERNIAWSKI

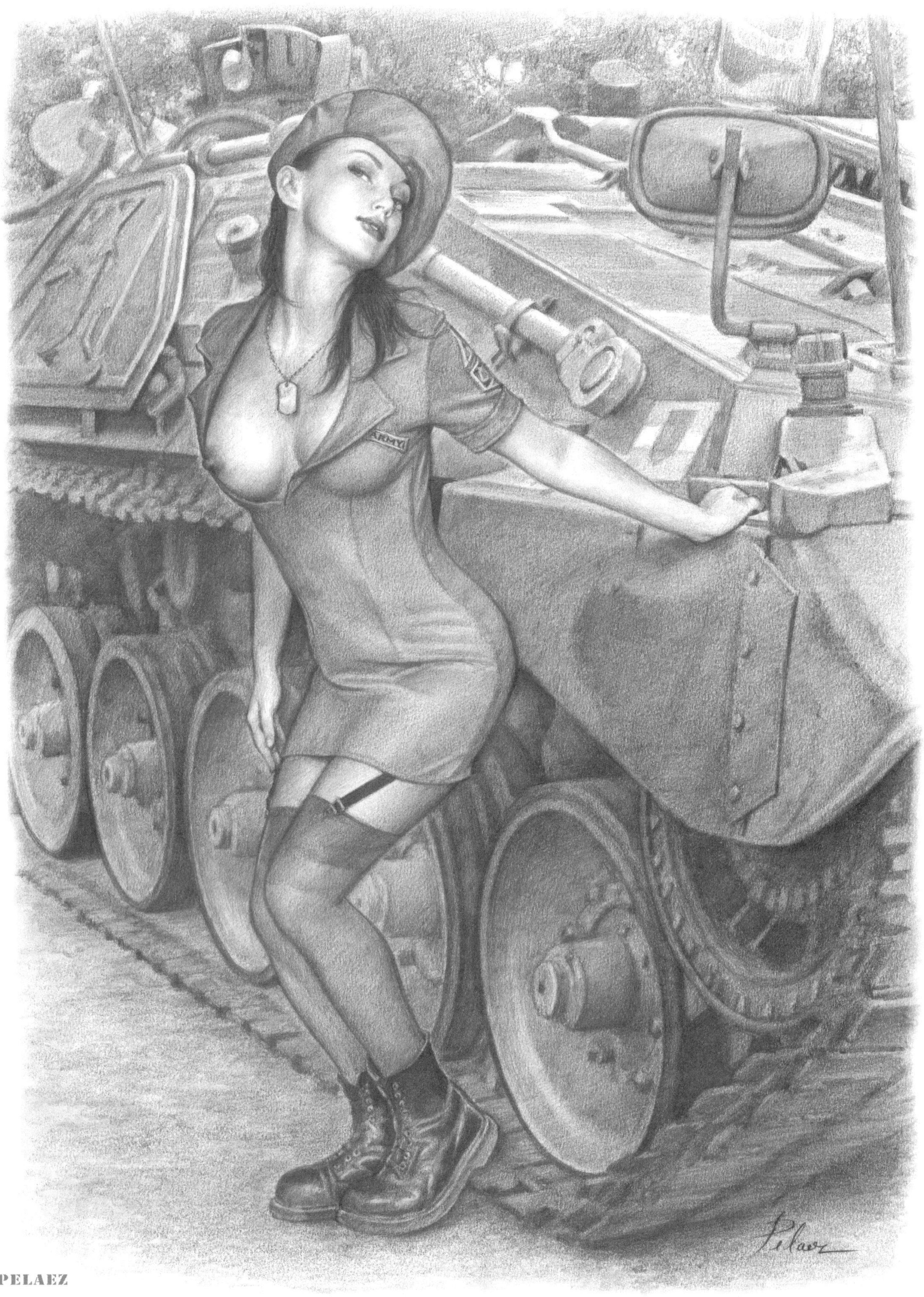
Pelaez

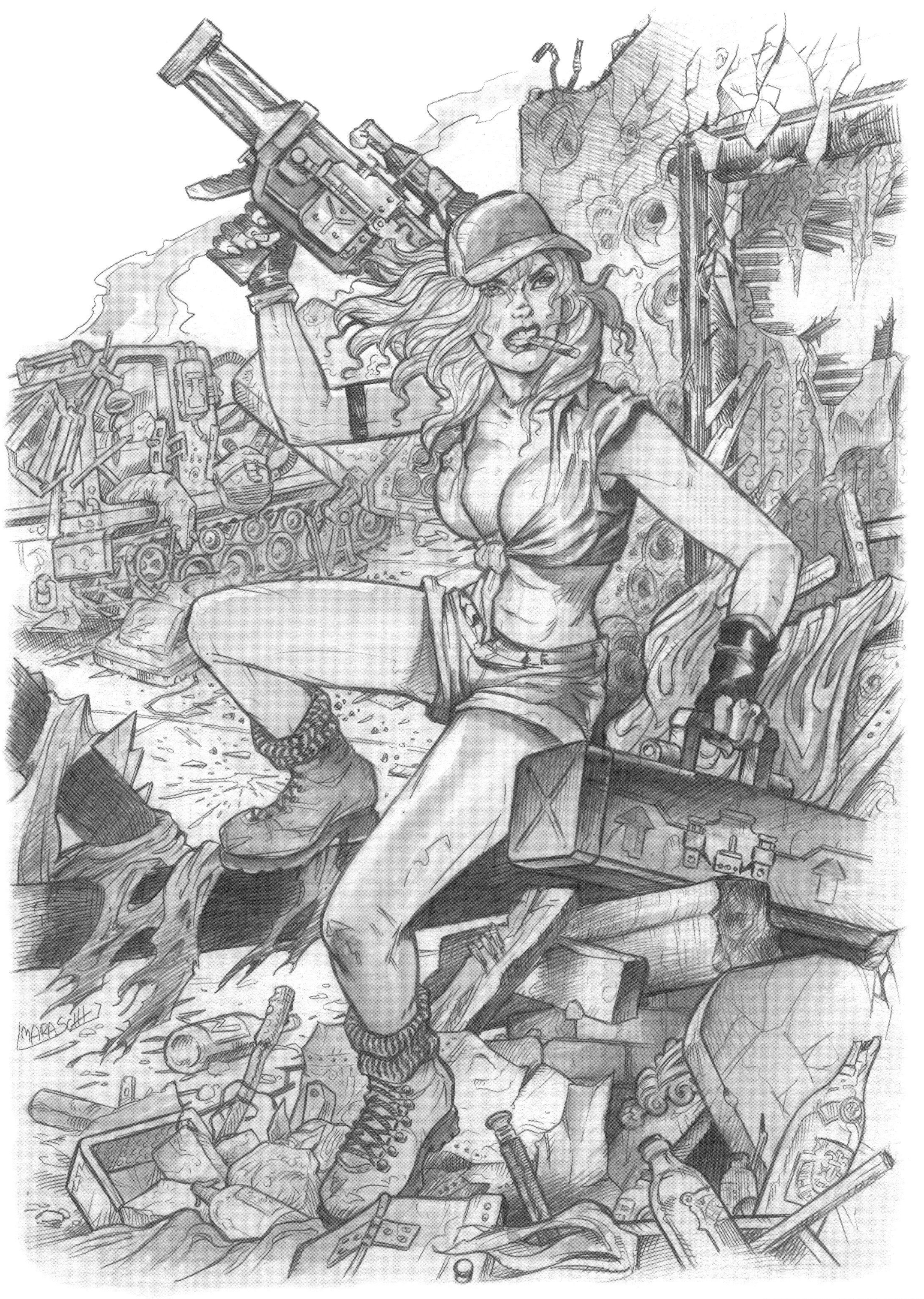

ANIBAL MARASCHI

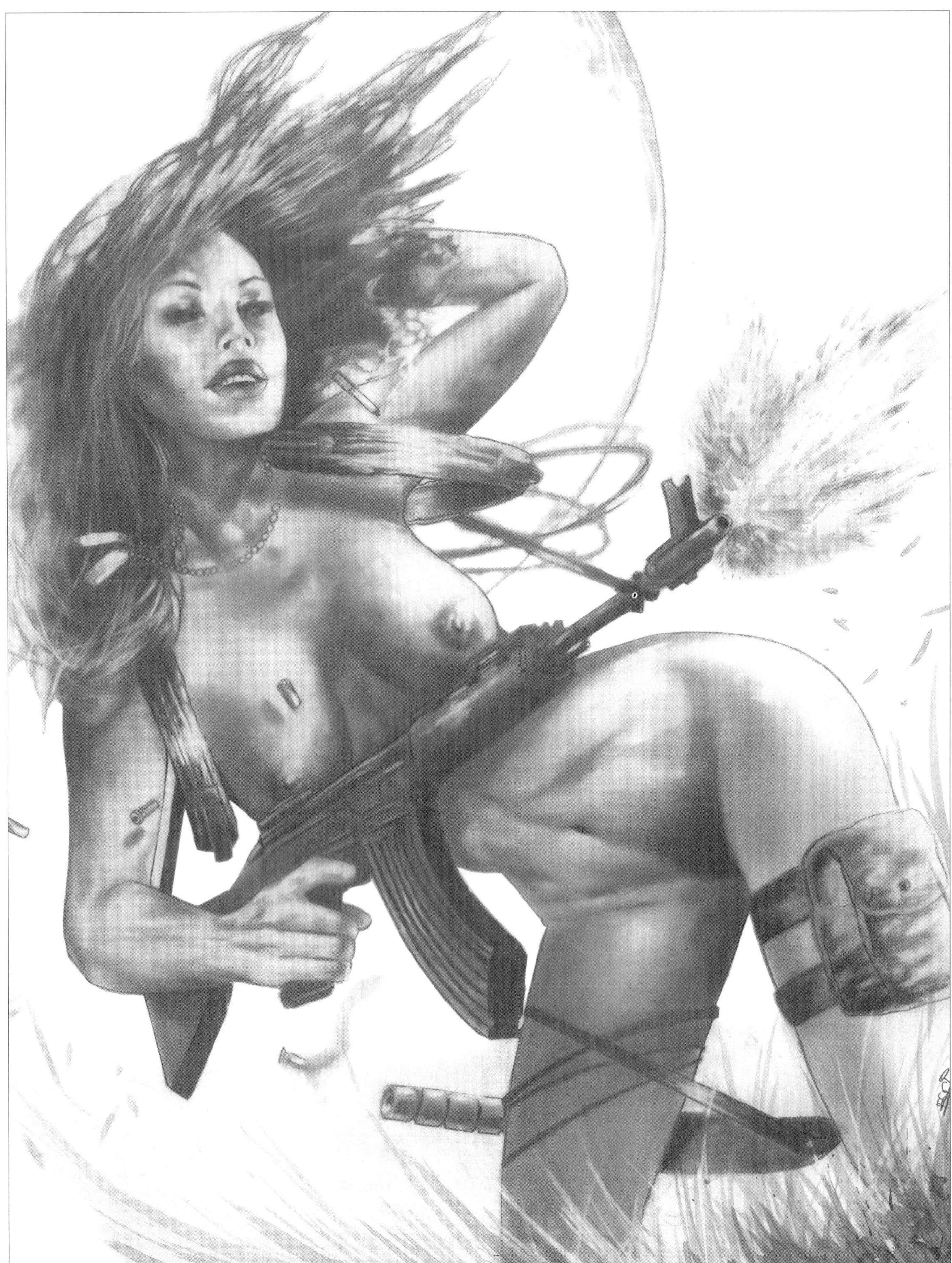

LUIS BUCI

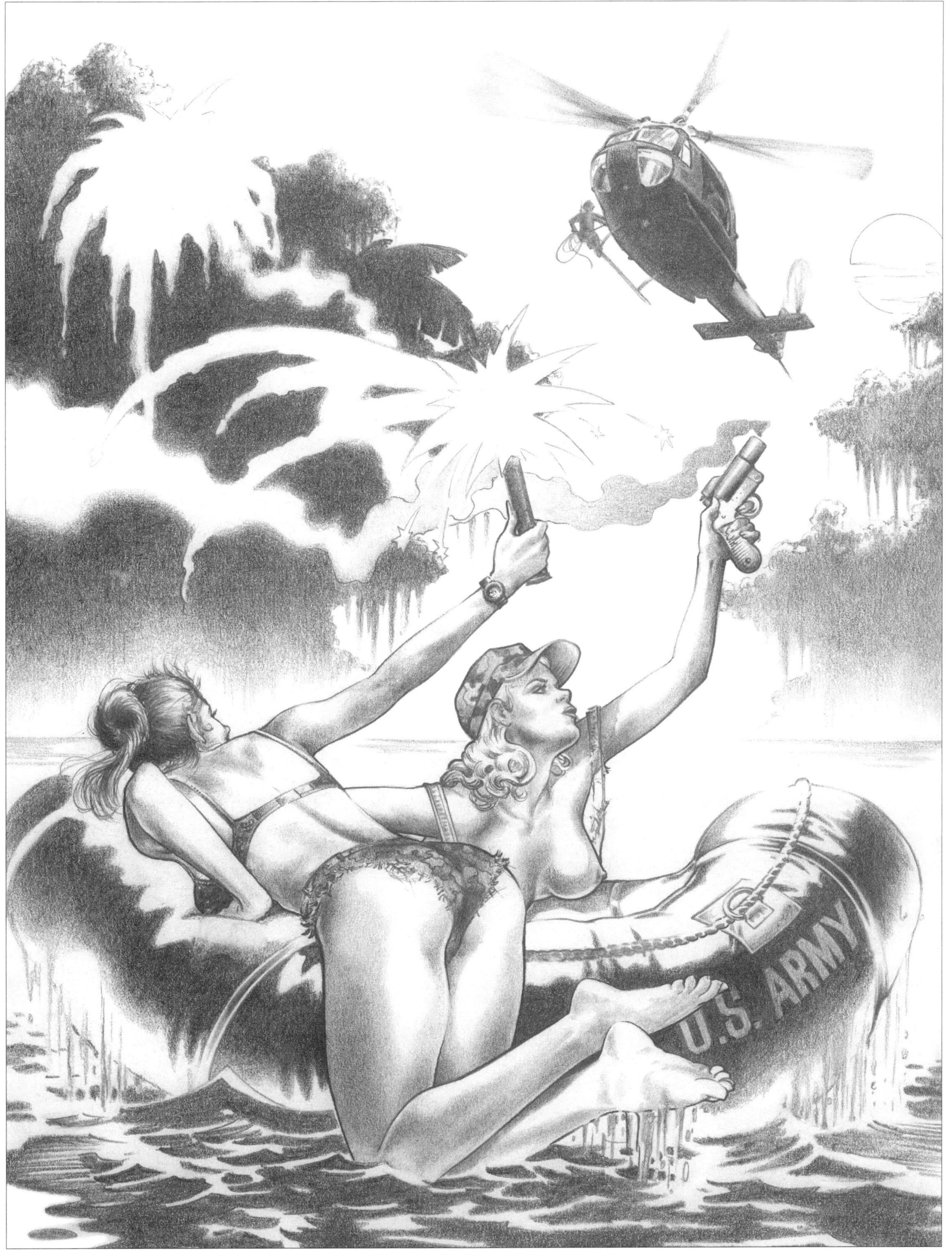

PERLA PILUCKI

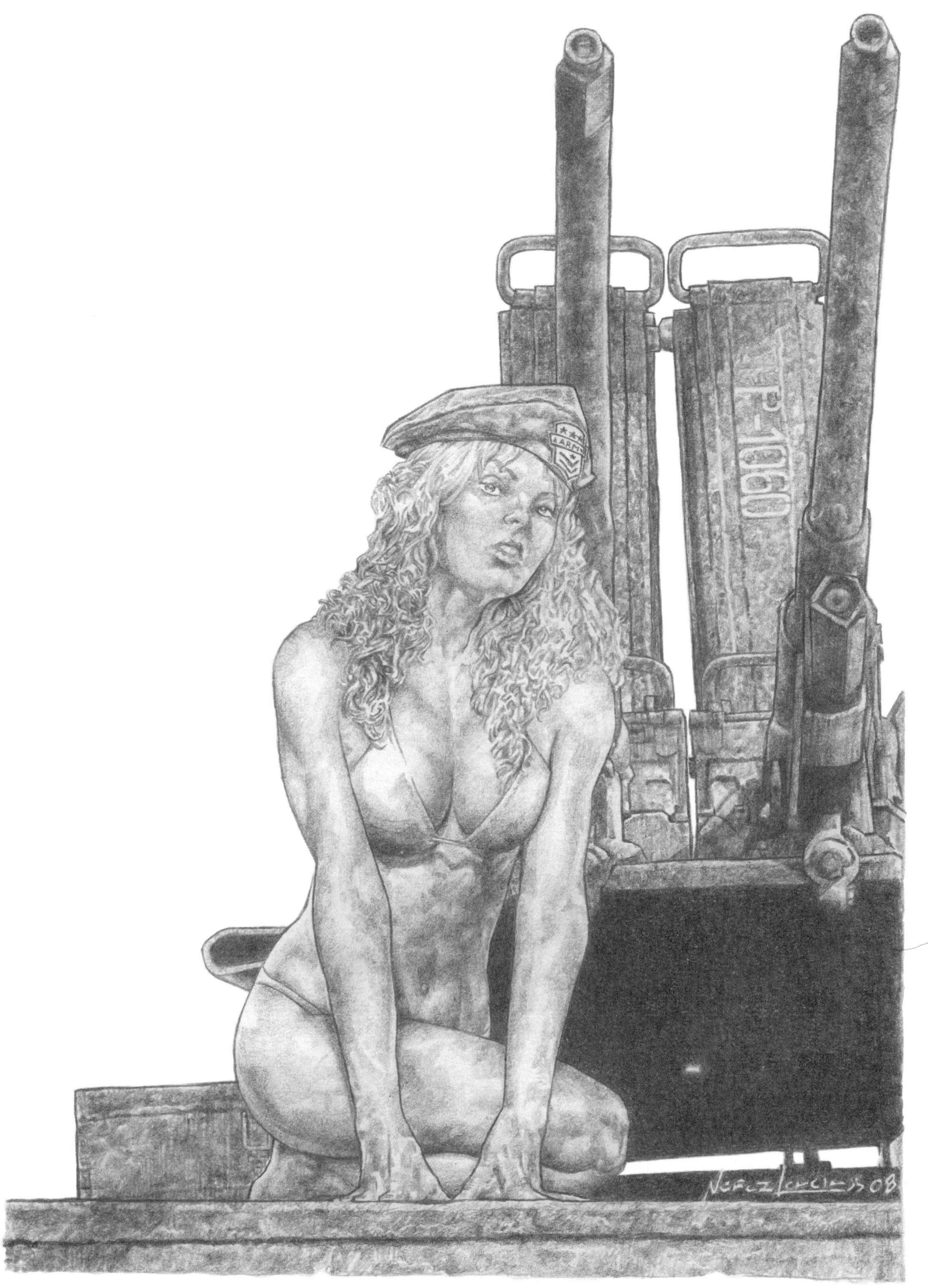

JUAN LENCINA

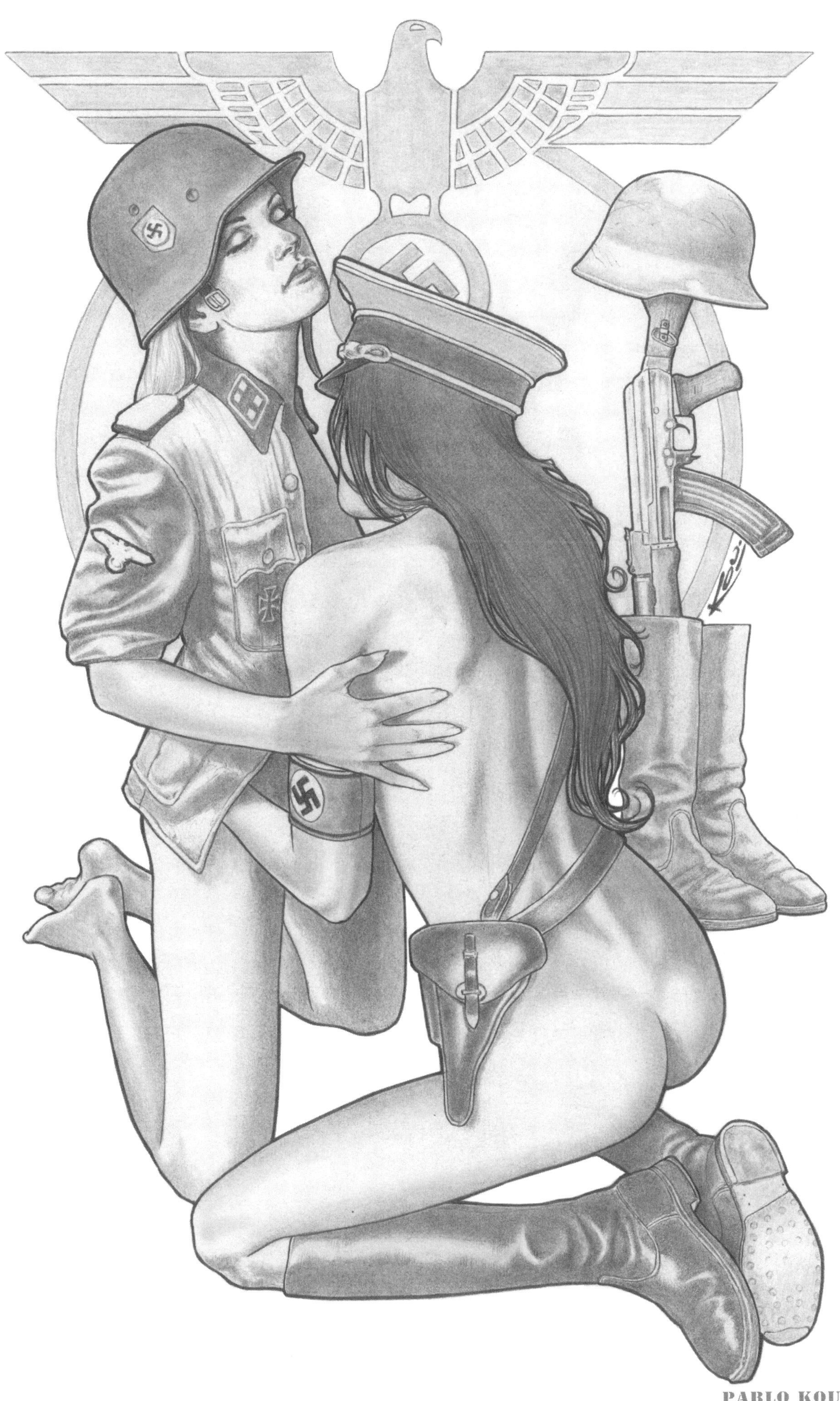

PABLO KOUSOVITIS

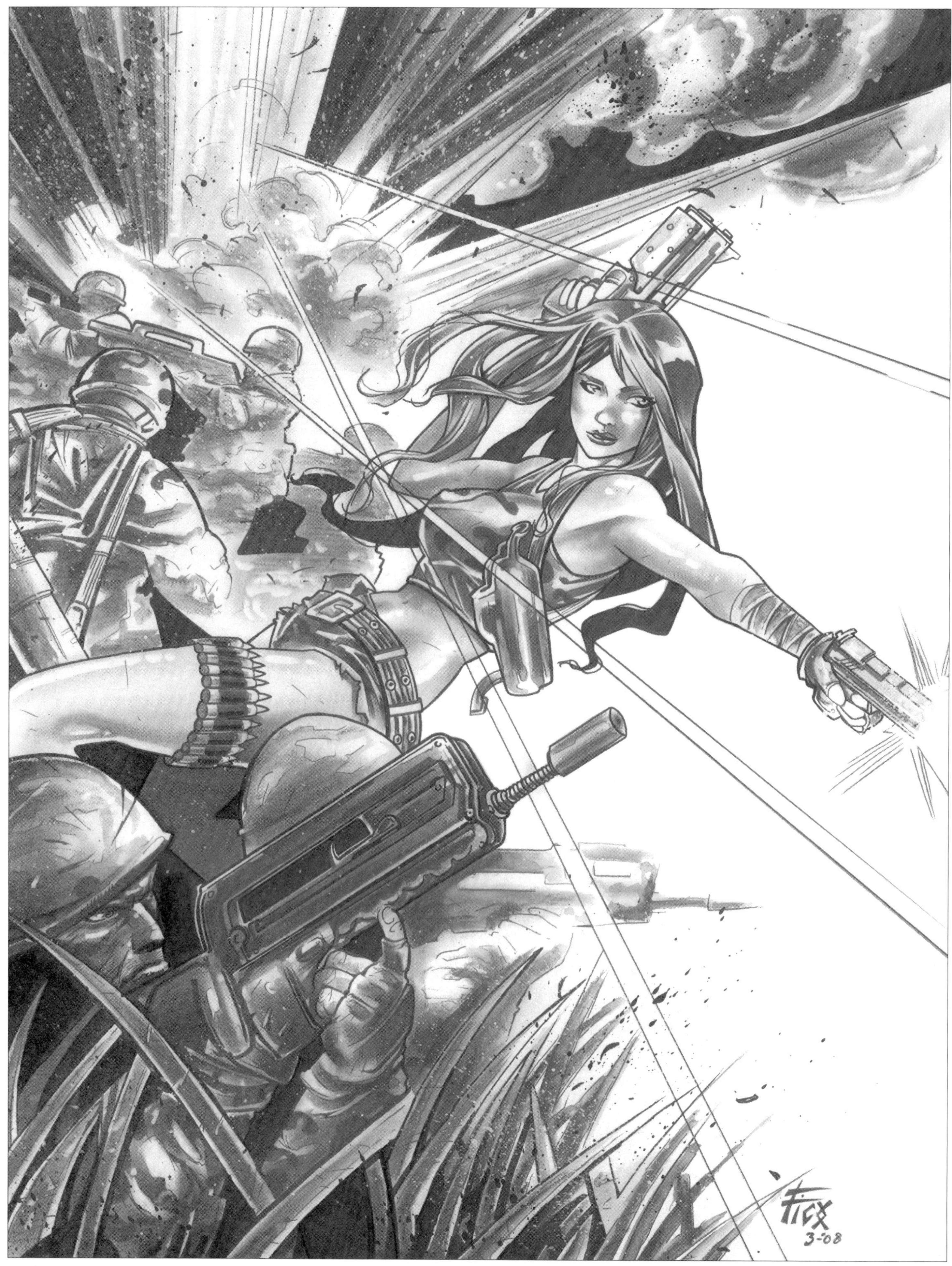

FEDERICO OSSIO

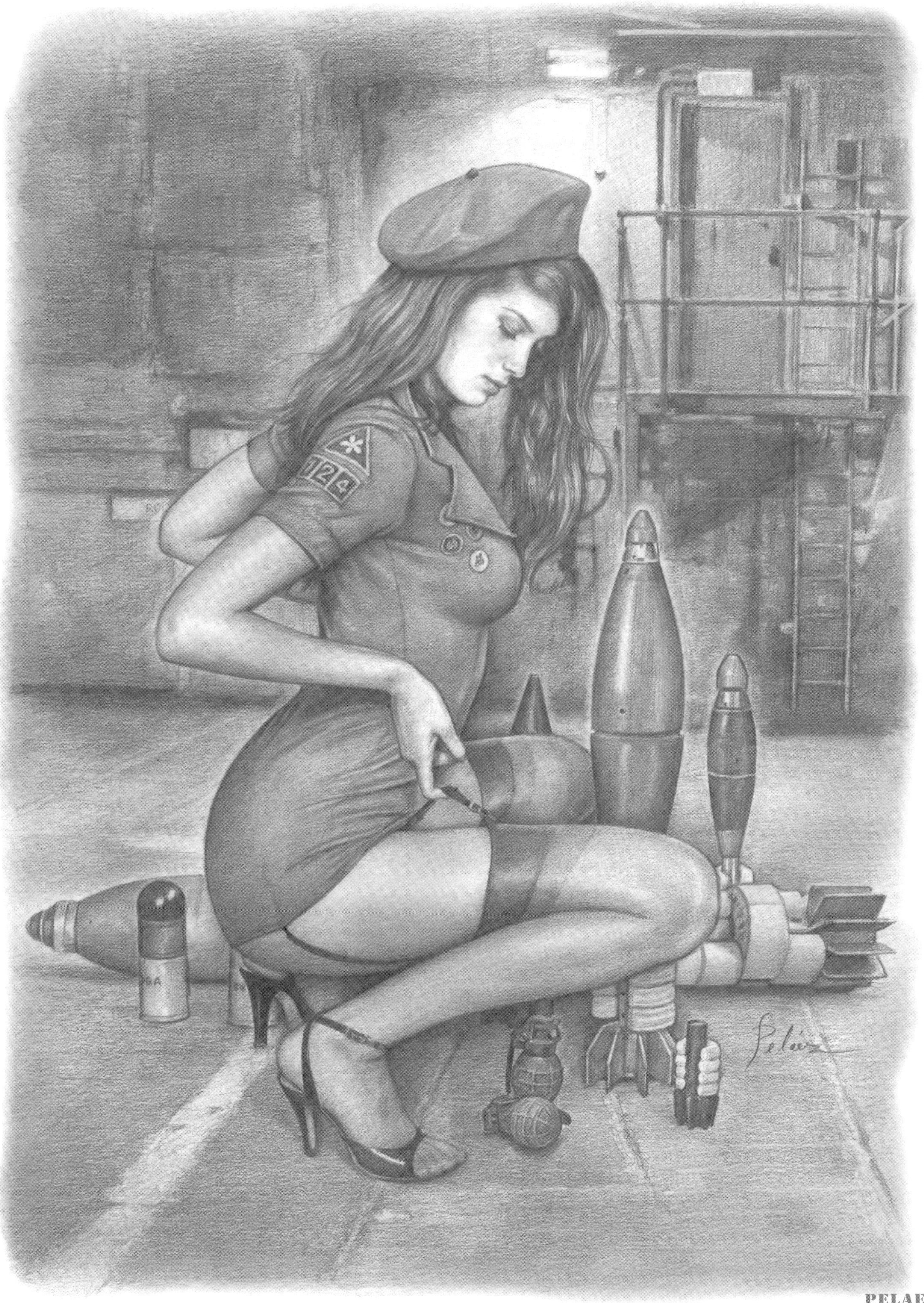

PELAEZ

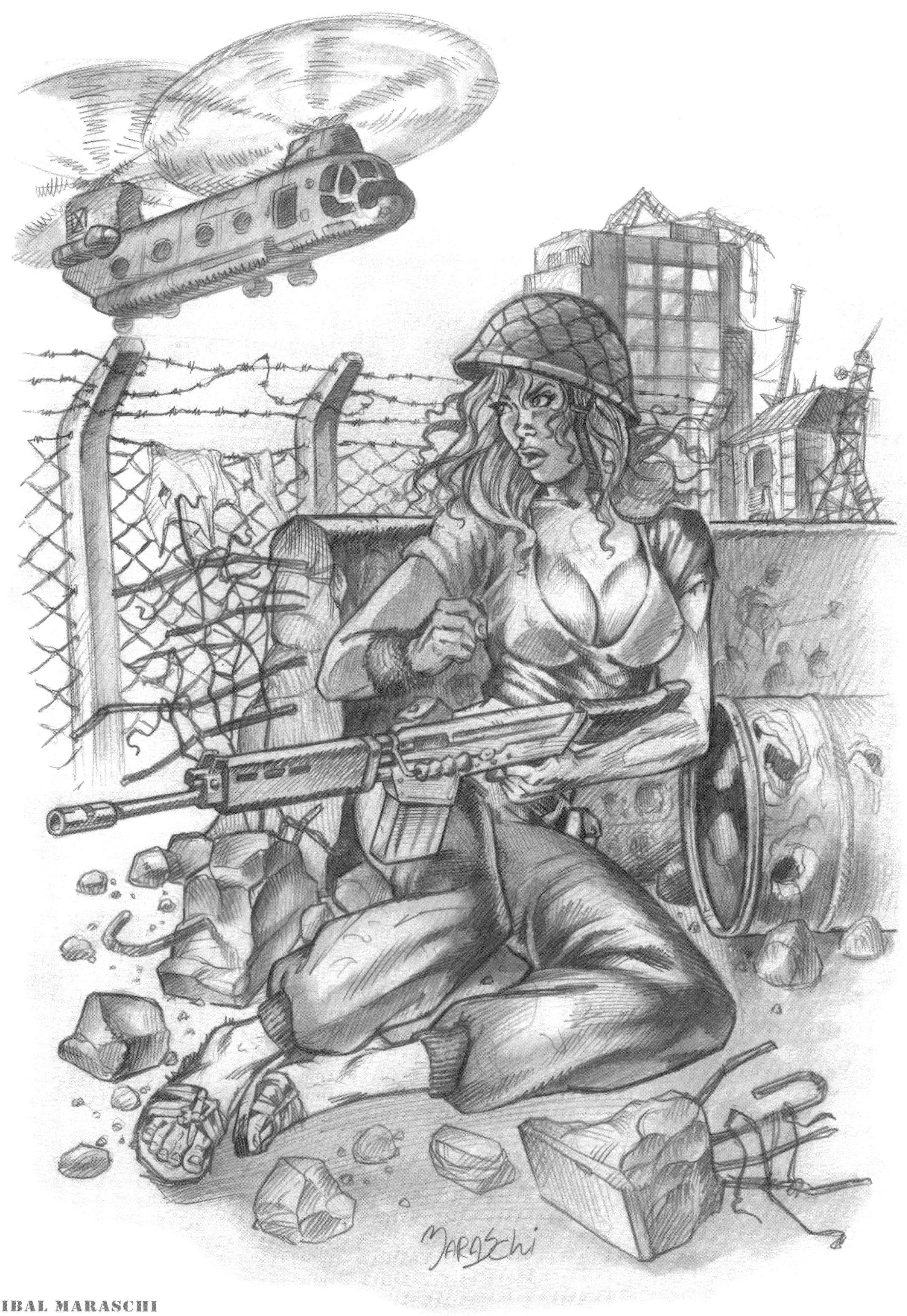

ANIBAL MARASCHI

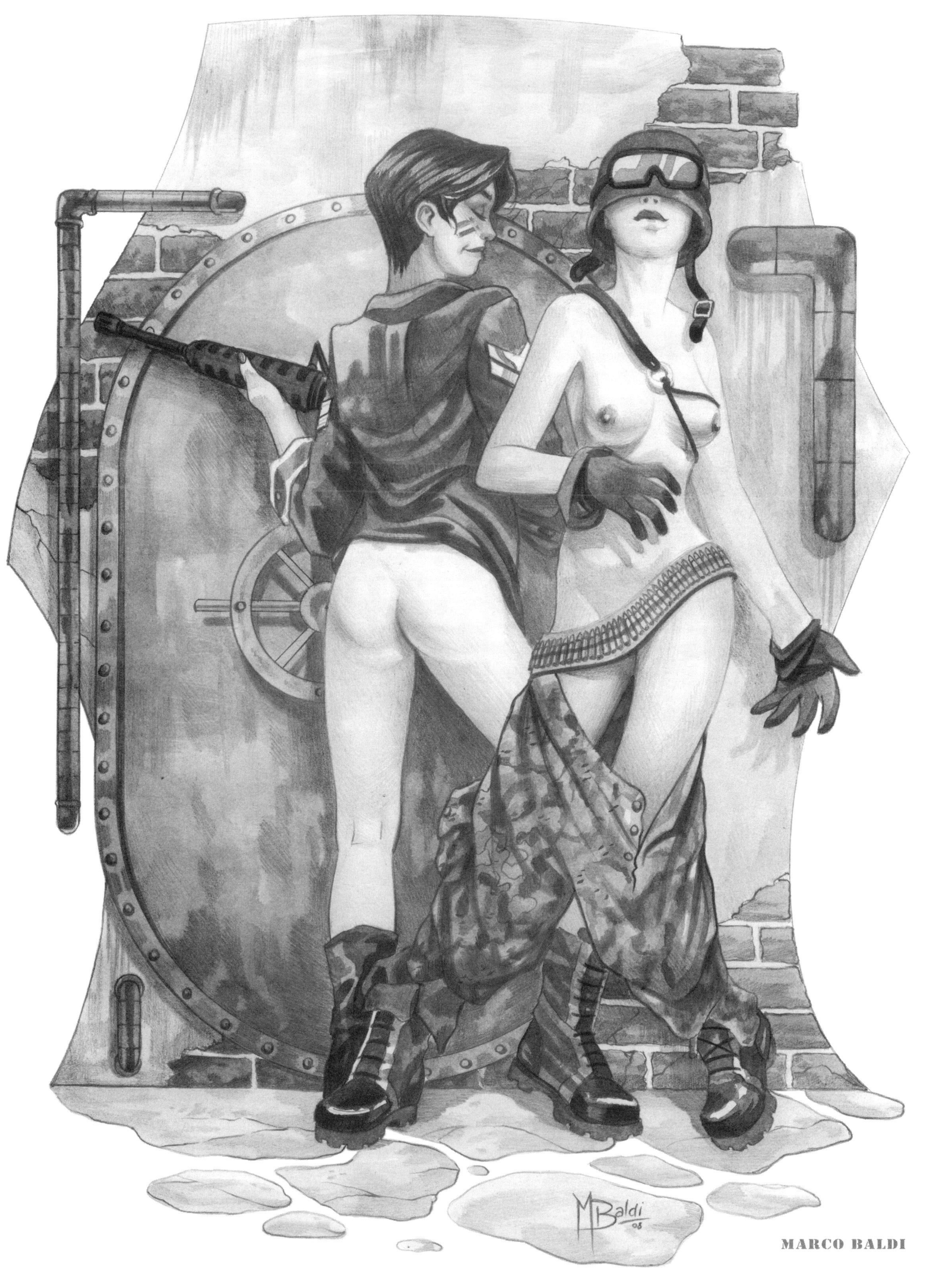

MARCO BALDI

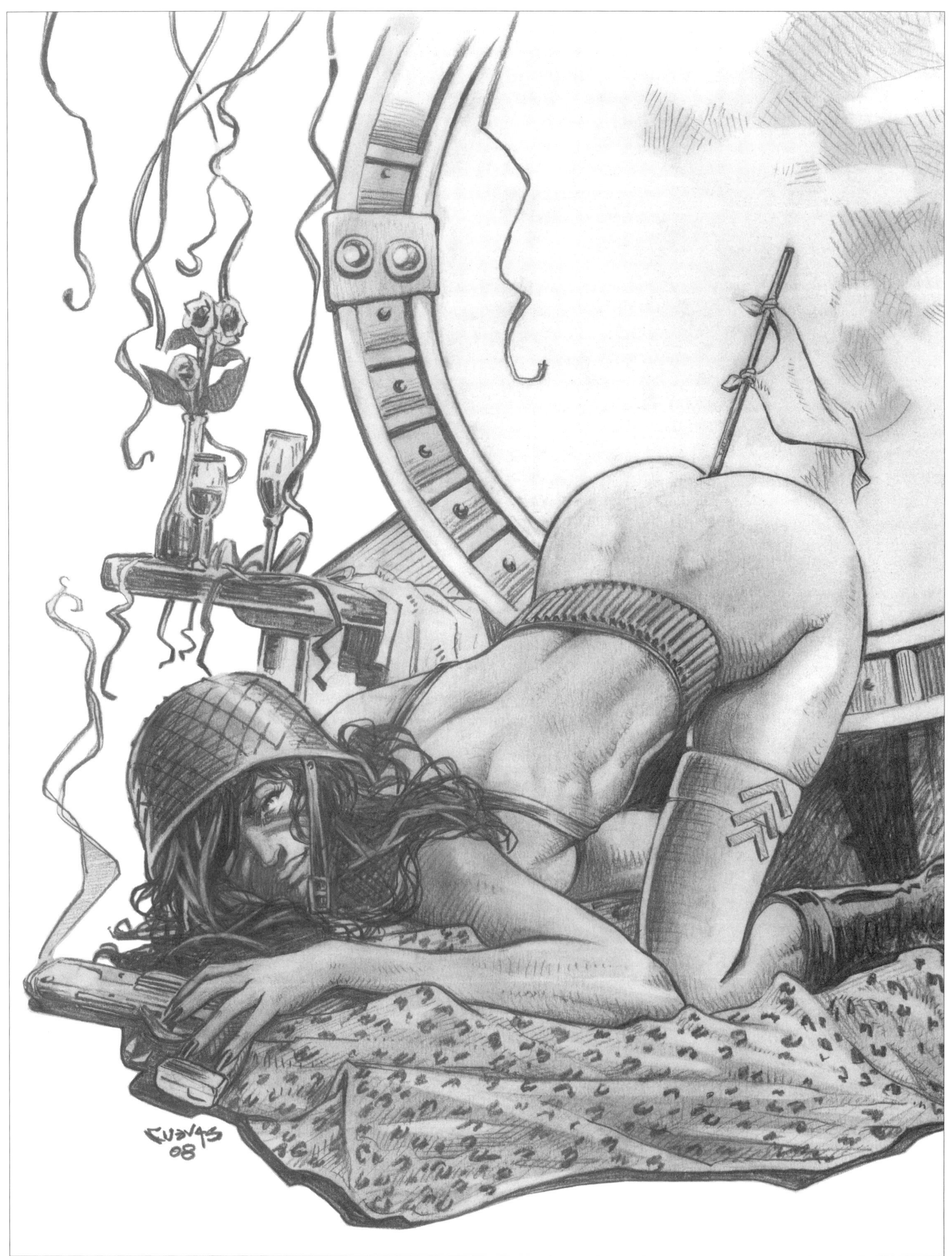

PEDRO CUEVAS

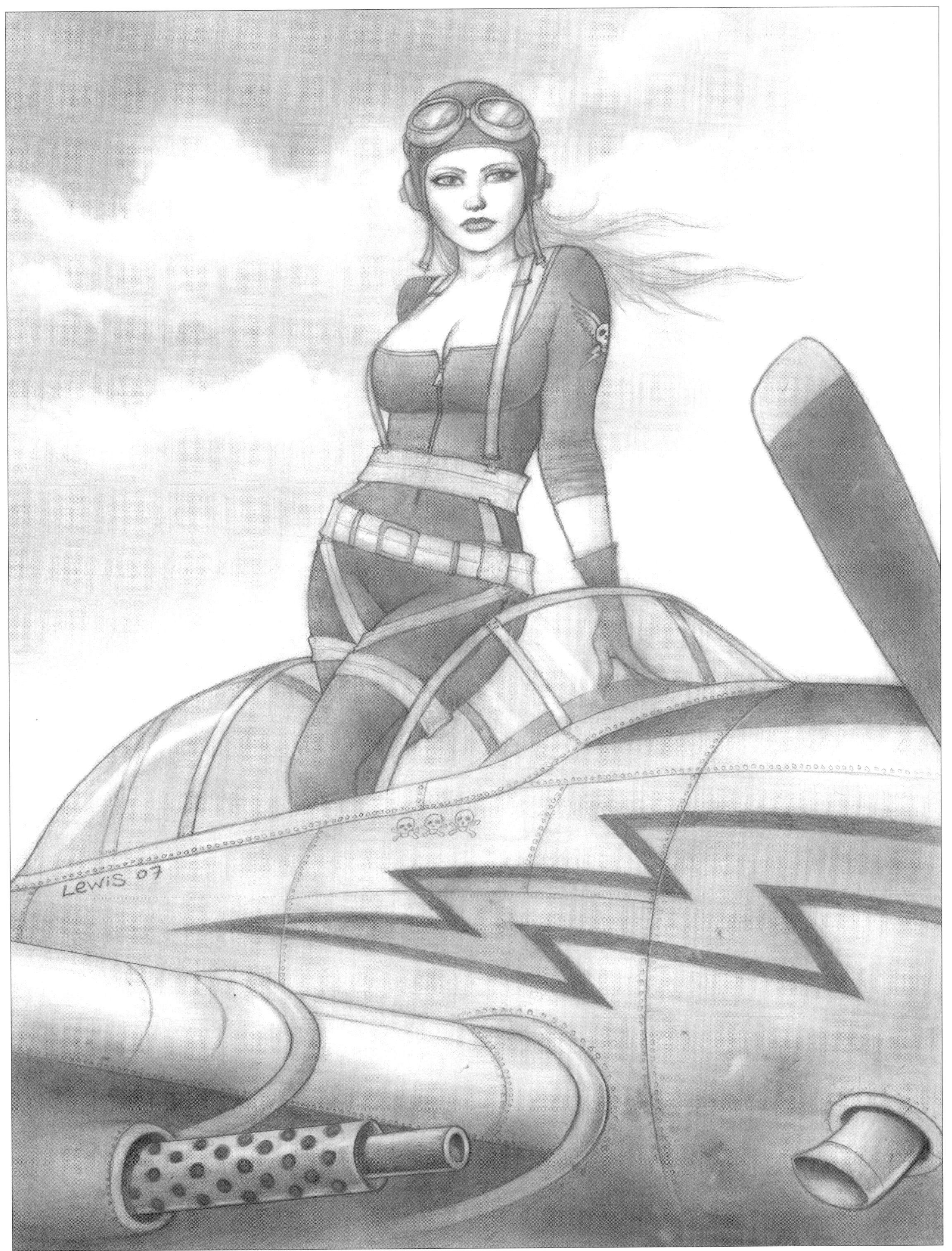

SCOTT LEWIS

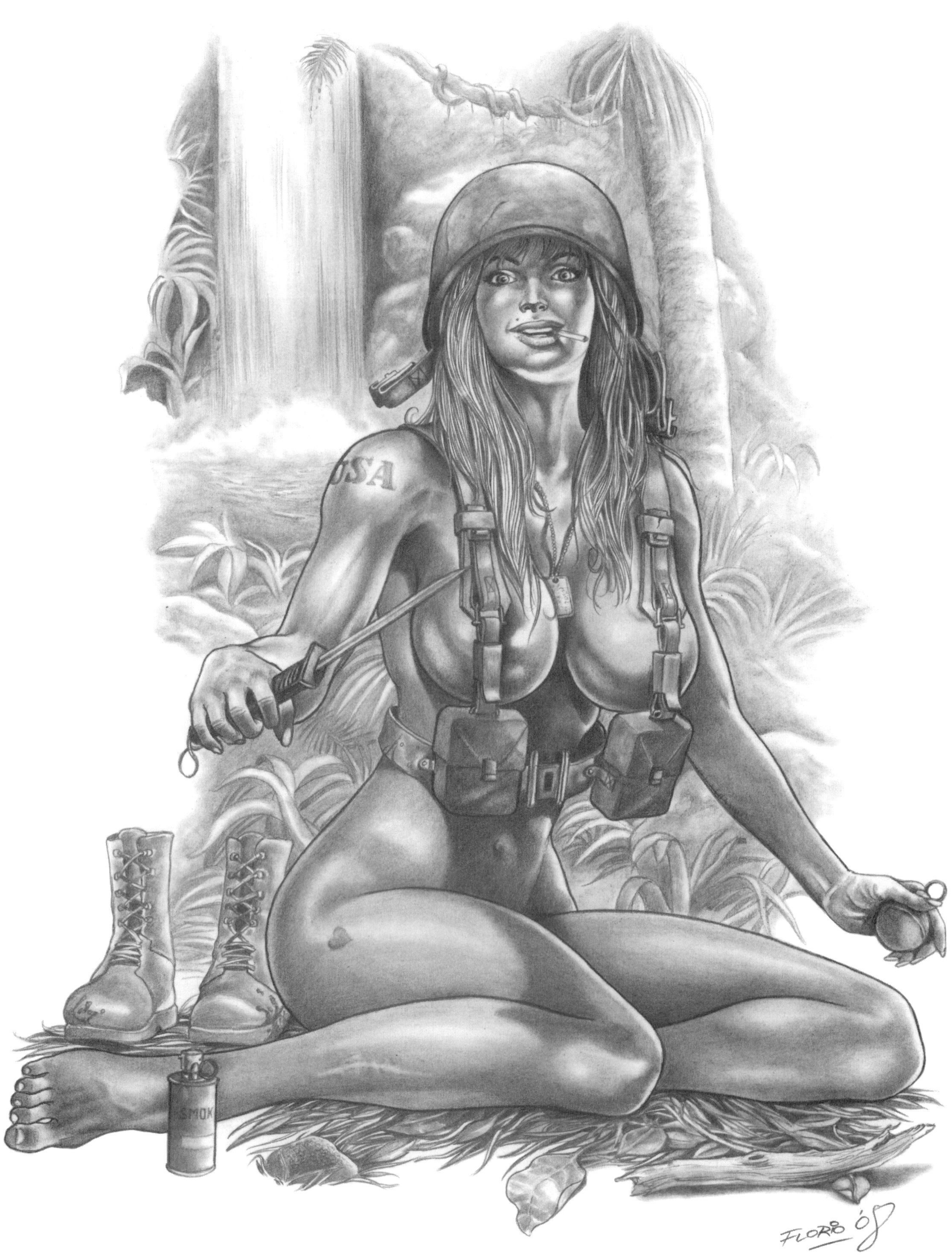

DIEGO FLORIO

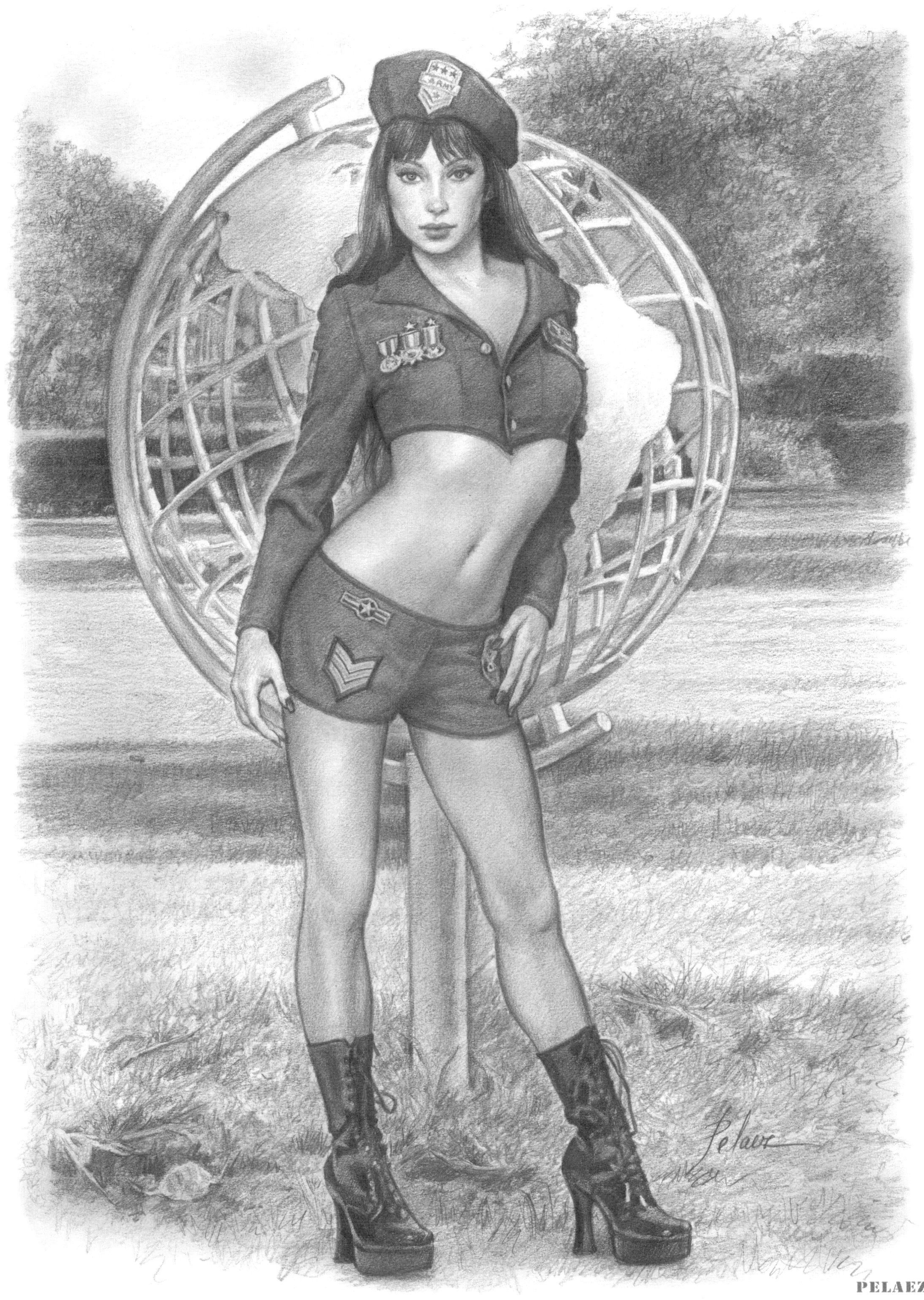

PELAEZ

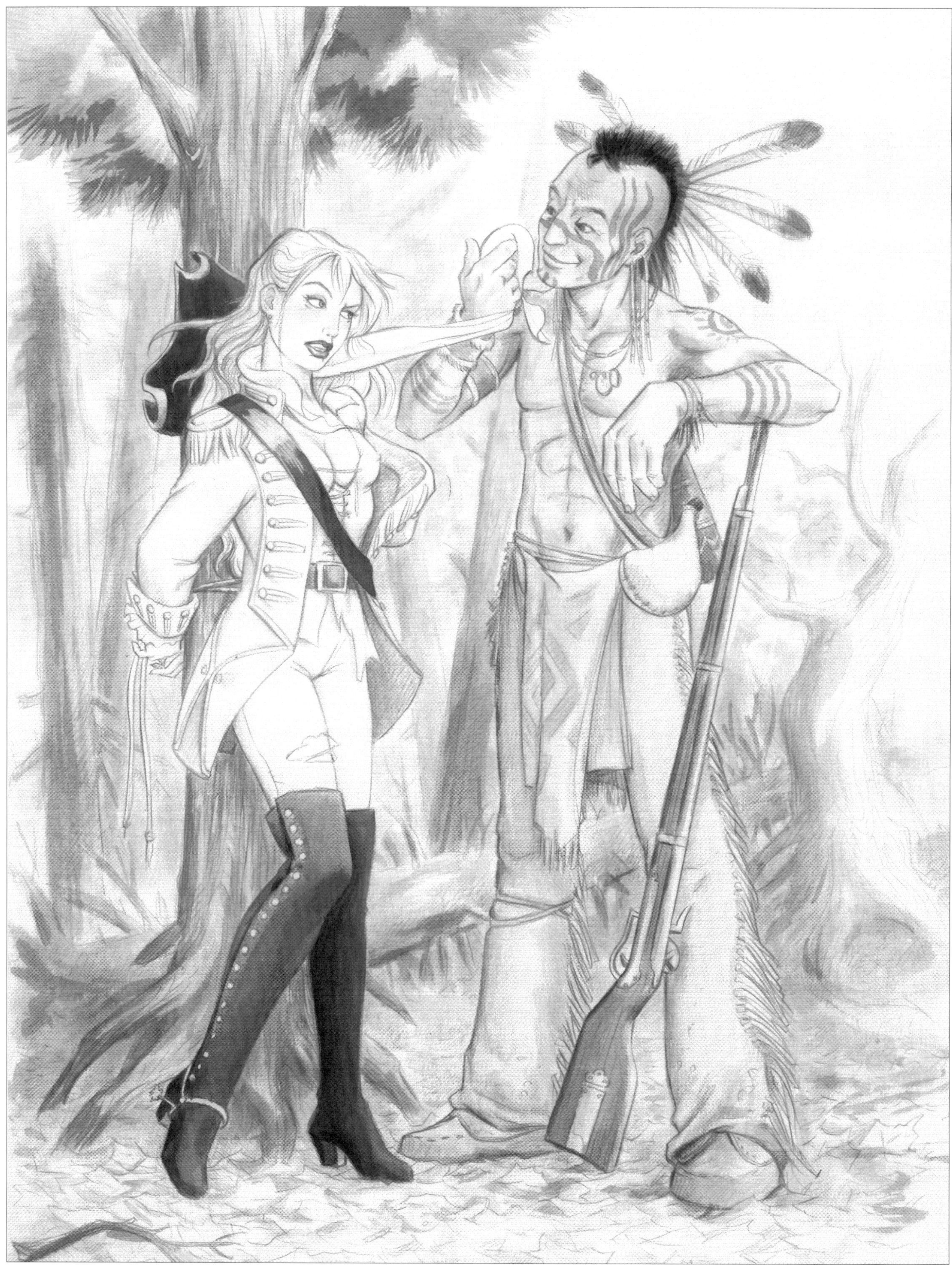

VICTOR AHMED

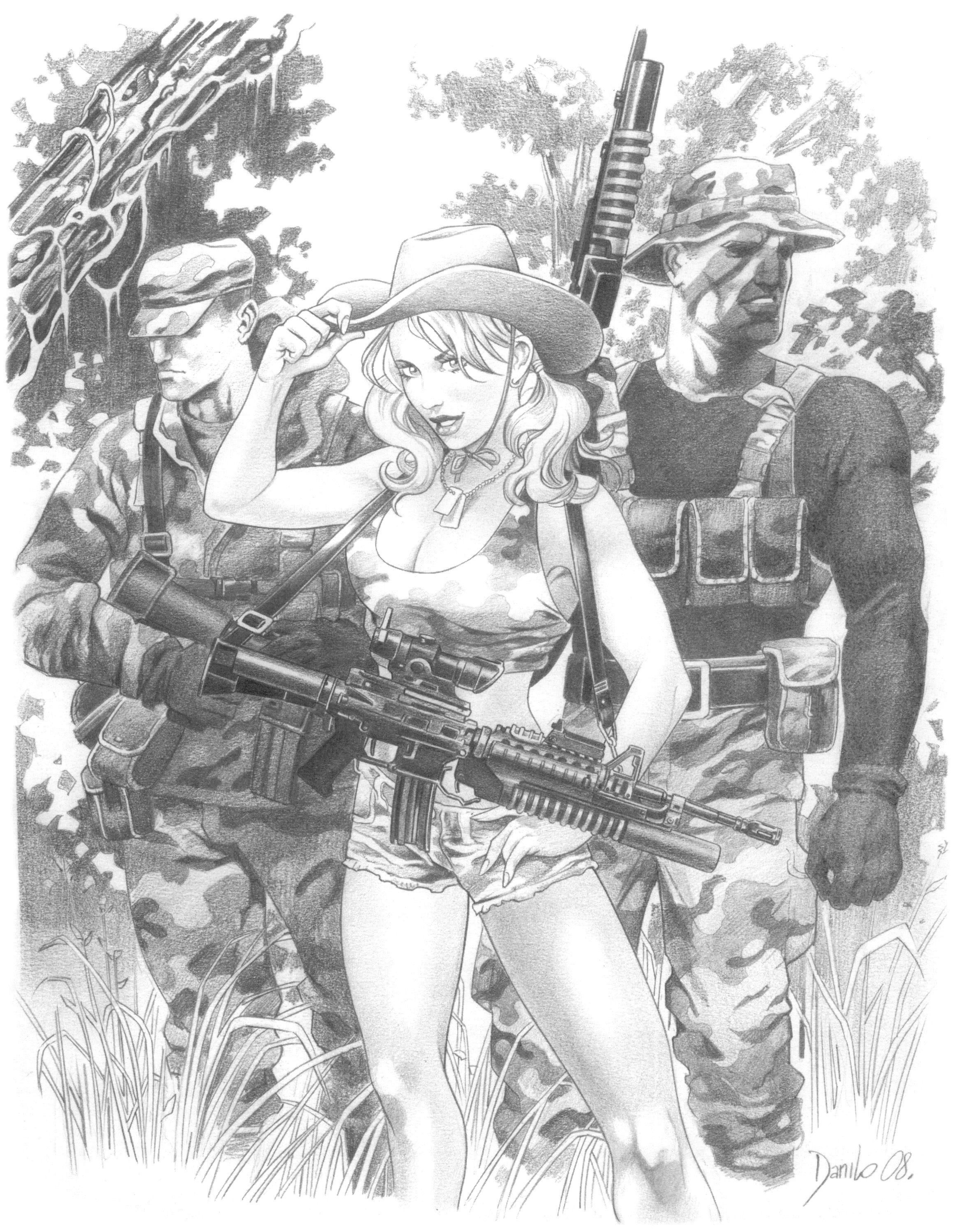

DANILO GUIDA

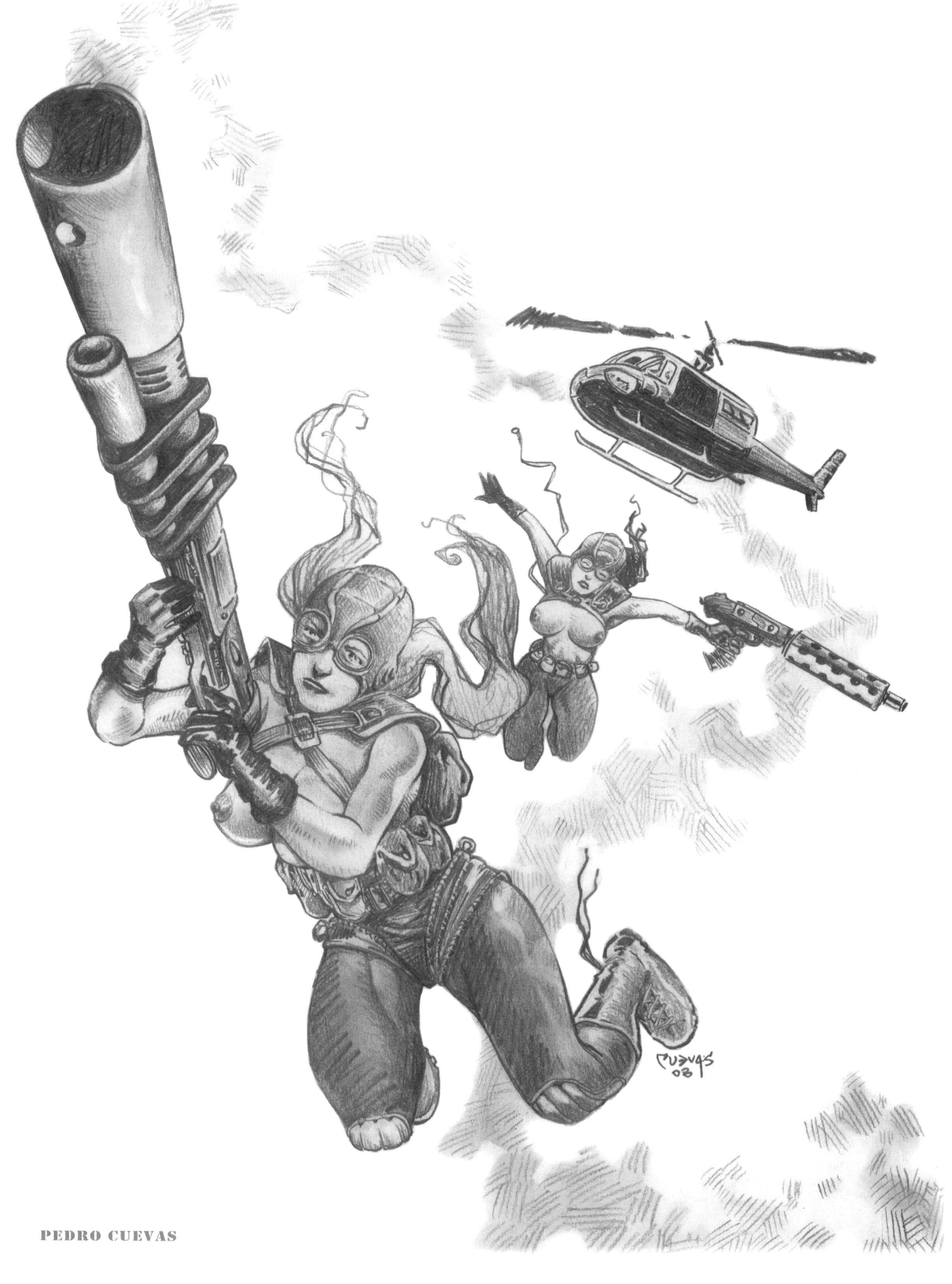

PEDRO CUEVAS

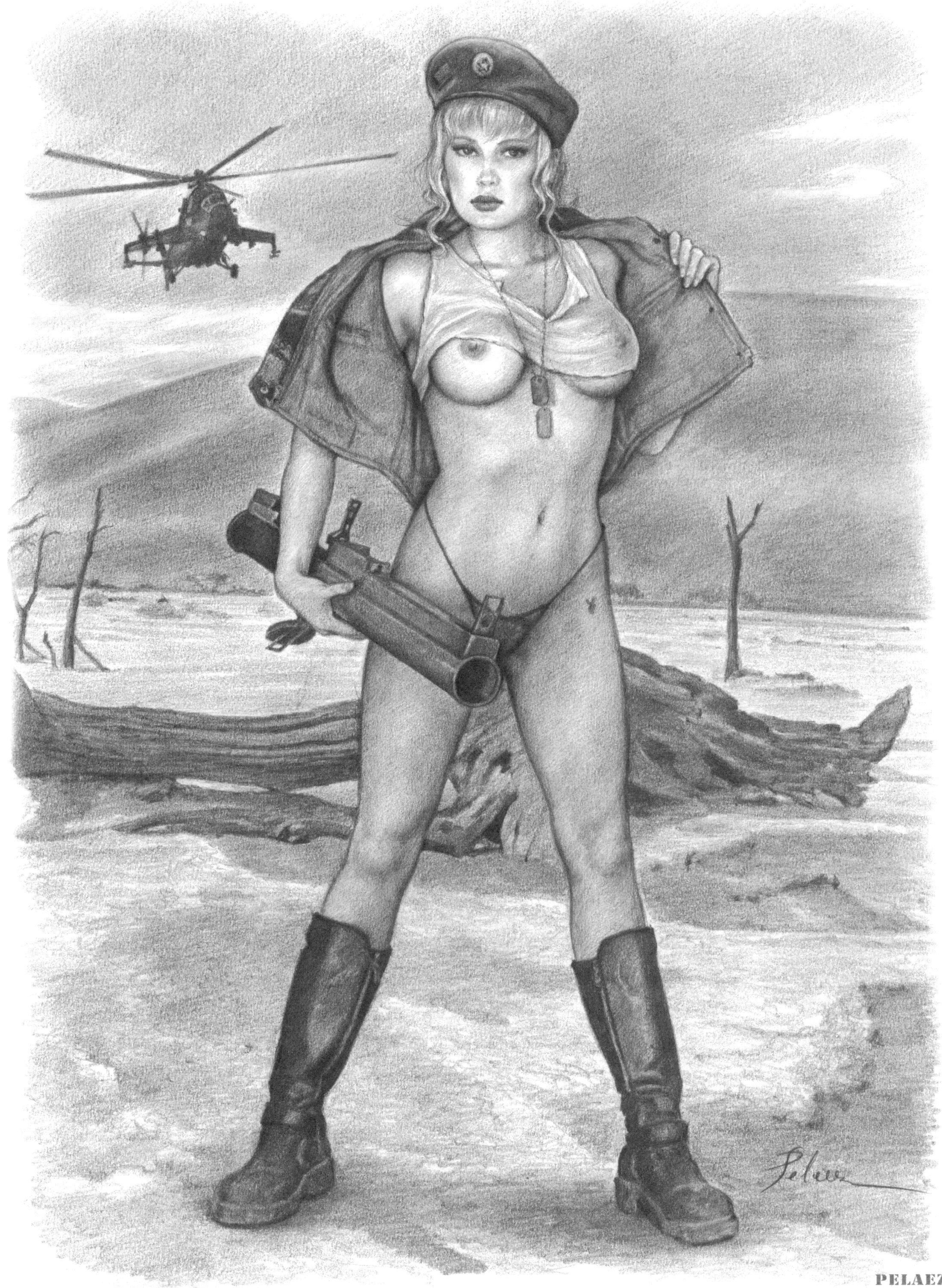

PELAEZ

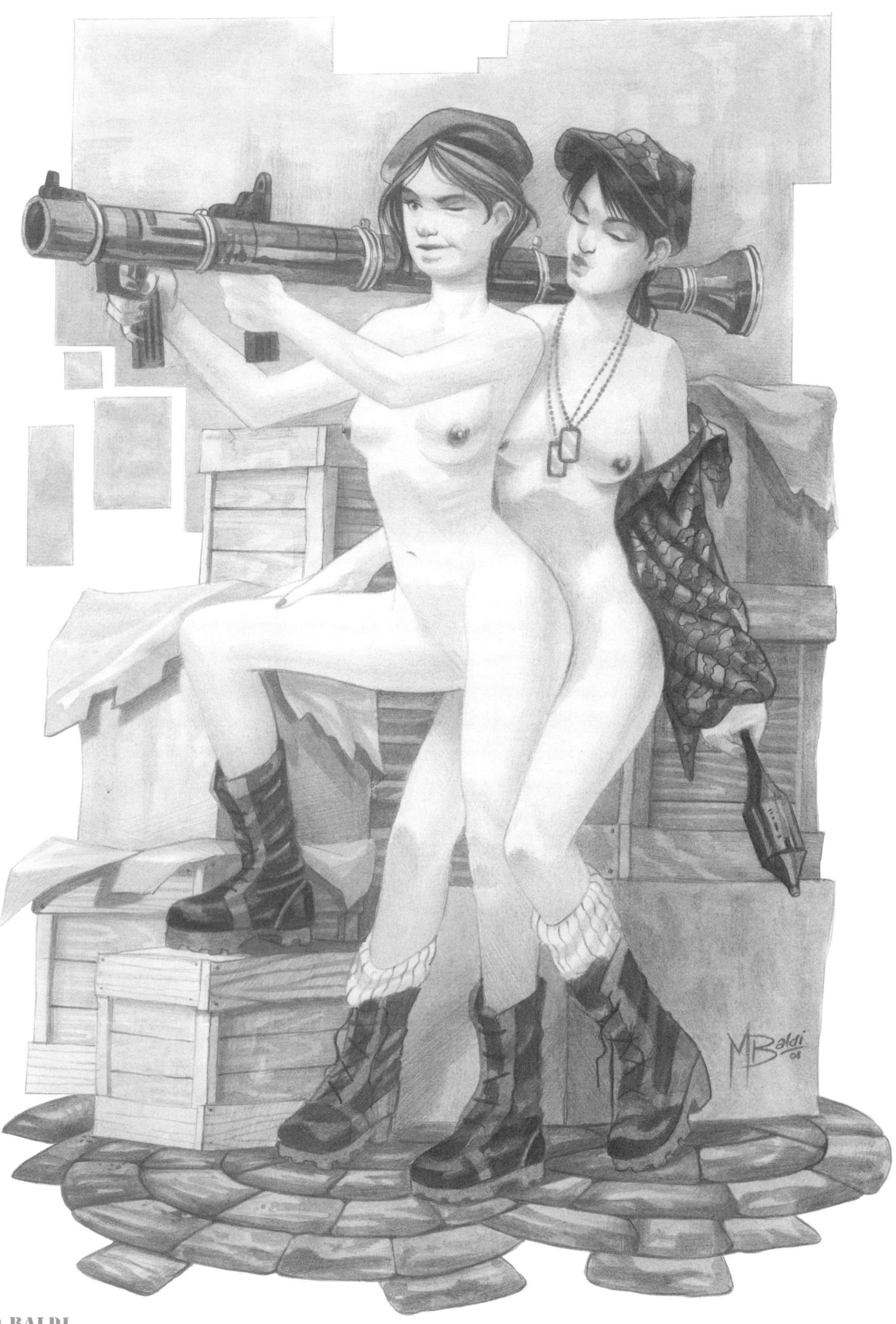

MARCO BALDI

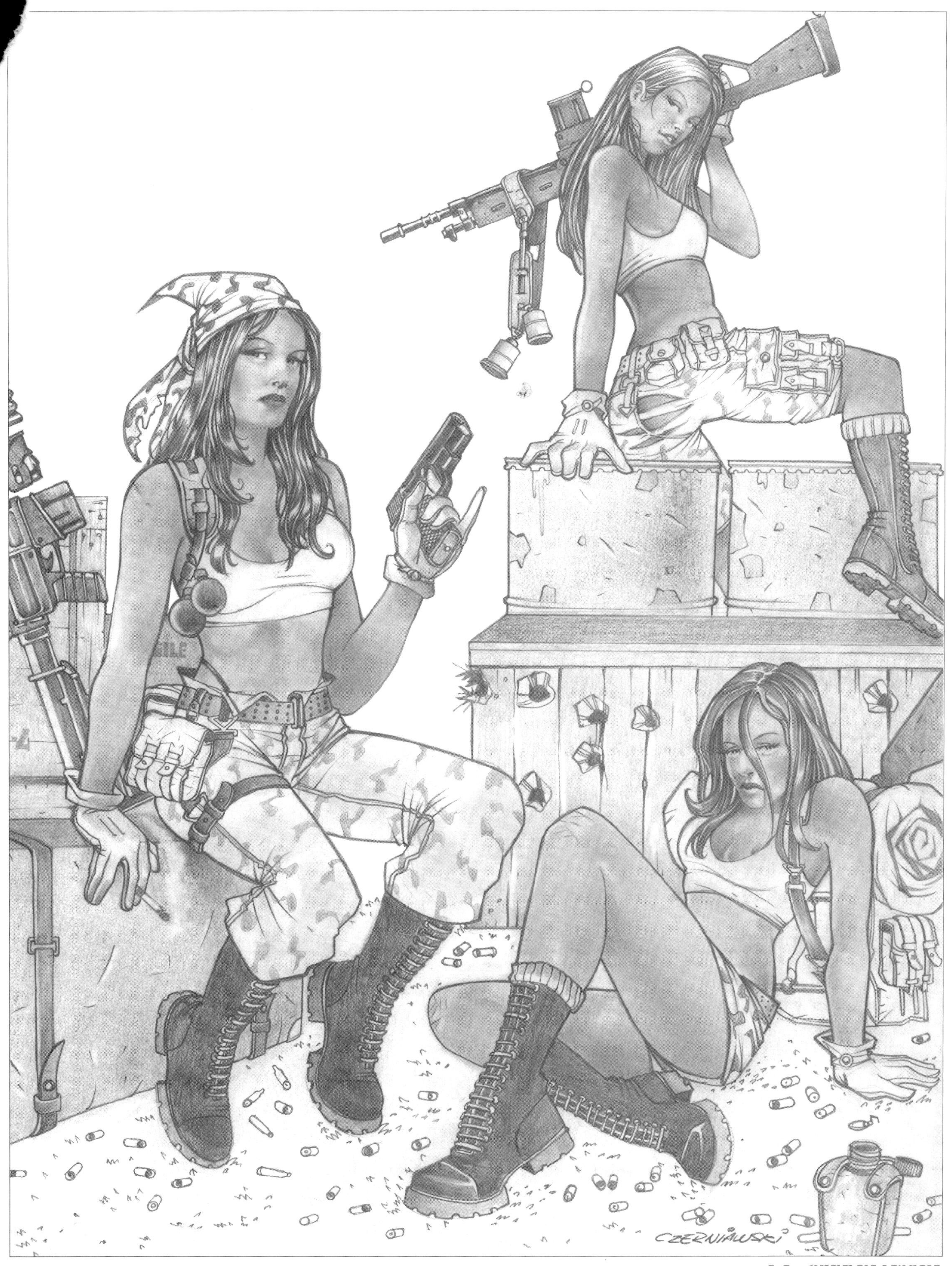

J.L. CZERNIAWSKI

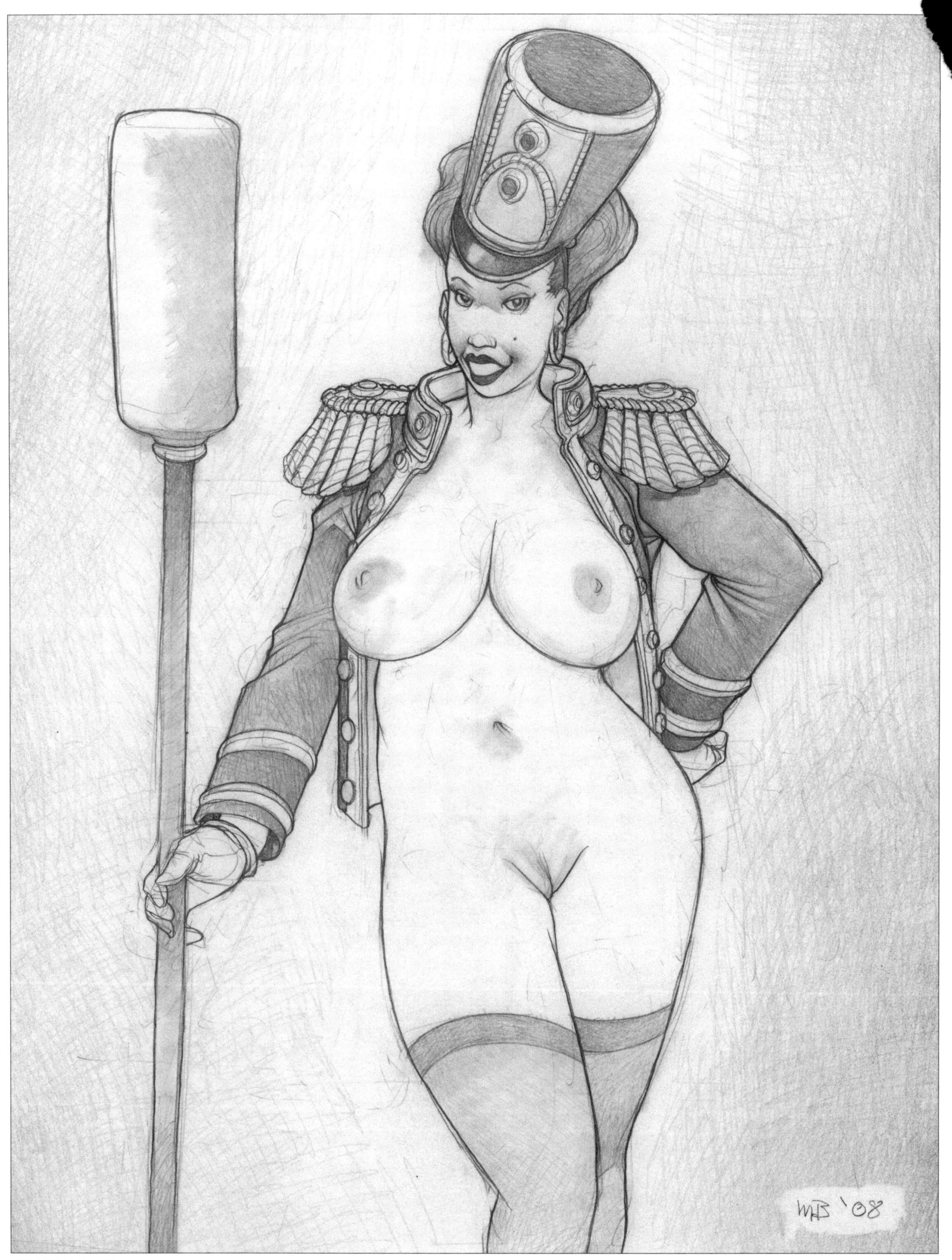

MITCH BYRD

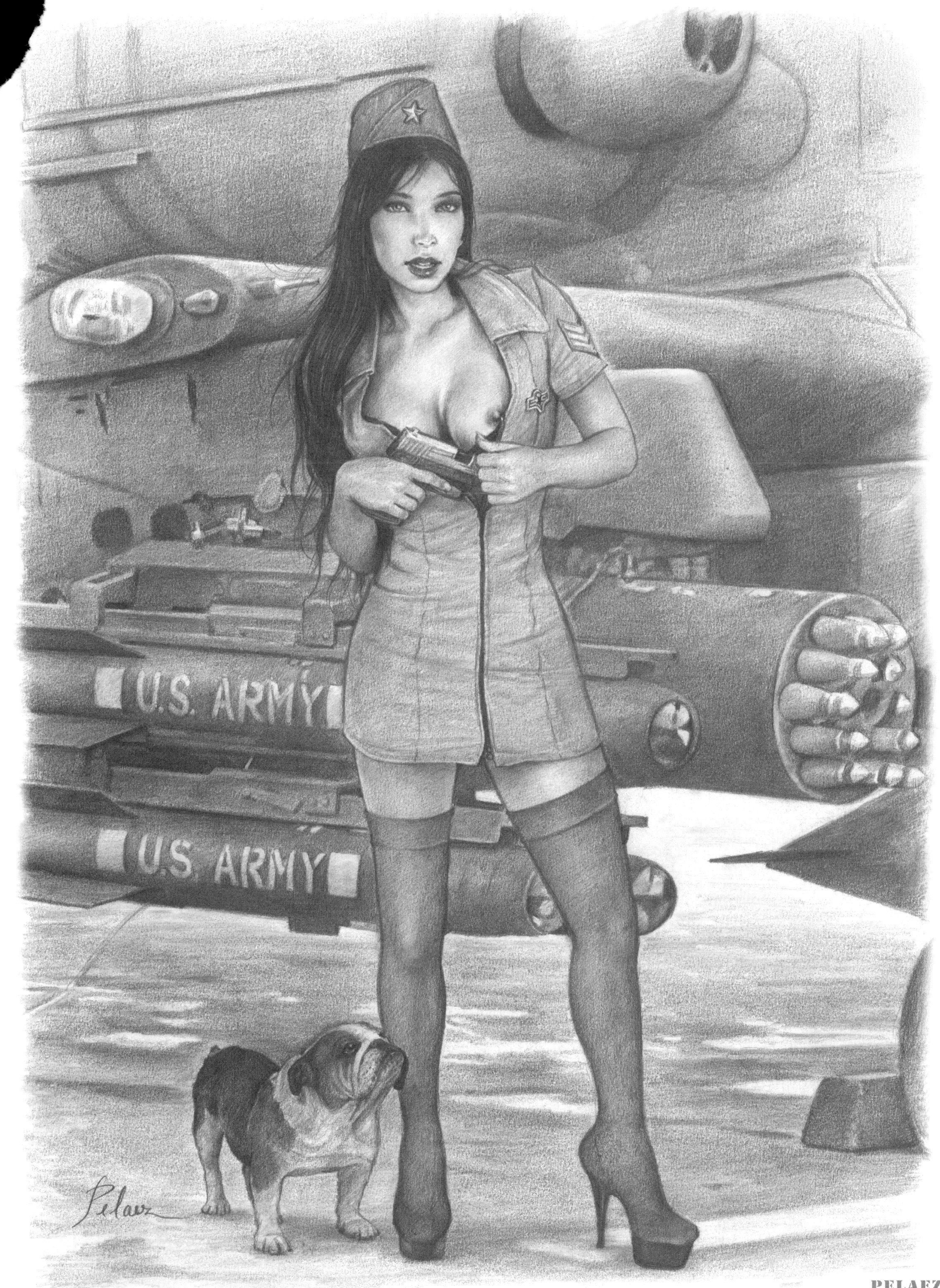

PELAEZ

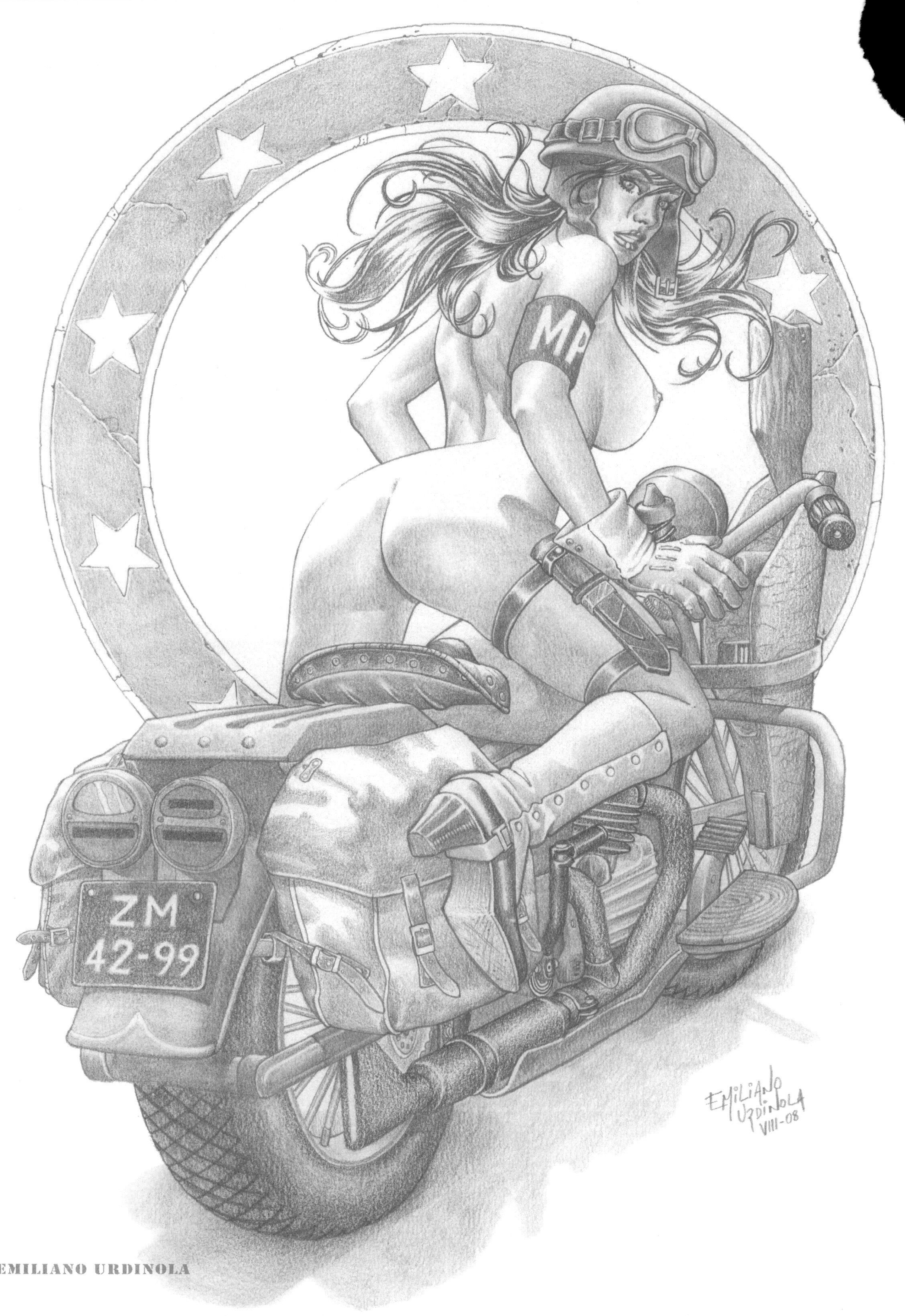

EMILIANO URDINOLA